Quick cooking
for
diabetes

A Pyramid Cooking Paperback

Quick cooking
for
diabetes

Louise Blair and Norma McGough

hamlyn

An Hachette UK Company
www.hachette.co.uk

A Pyramid paperback from Hamlyn

First published in Great Britain in 2002 by Hamlyn
a division of Octopus Publishing Group Limited
2–4 Heron Quays, London E14 4JP
www.octopusbooksusa.com

Revised editions published in 2005 and 2008

This edition published 2009

Distributed in the U.S. and Canada by Octopus Books USA:
c/o Hachette Book Group USA
237 Park Avenue
New York NY 10017

This material was previously published as *Quick Cooking for Diabetes*

ISBN: 978-0-600-62030-3

Printed and bound in China

10 9 8 7 6 5 4 3 2 1

The publisher has taken all reasonable care in the preparation of this book but the information it contains is not intended to take the place of treatment by a qualified medical practitioner.

NOTES
Ovens should be preheated to the specified temperature. If using a fan-assisted oven, follow the manufacturer's instructions for adjusting the time and temperature. Broilers should also be preheated.

A few recipes include nuts and nut derivatives. Anyone with a known nut allergy must avoid these.

Free-range medium eggs should be used unless otherwise stated.
The Food and Drug Administration advises that eggs should not be consumed raw. It is prudent for more vulnerable people such as pregnant and nursing mothers, invalids, the elderly, babies, and young children to avoid uncooked or lightly cooked dishes made with eggs.

Meat and poultry should be cooked thoroughly. To test if poultry is cooked, pierce the flesh through the thickest part with a skewer or fork—the juices should run clear, never pink or red.

All the recipes in this book have been analyzed by a State Registered Dietitian. The analysis refers to each serving.

  Suitable for vegetarians

All recipes serve 4

Contents

Introduction

If you have diabetes, you might think that there are certain foods that you can't eat, or that you can't enjoy social occasions in the same way as someone who doesn't have diabetes. This is not necessarily the case: in this book you will learn how to make changes to your choice of food, your eating habits and cooking, to help you manage your diabetes more effectively and live life to the full.

The recipes have been allocated their appropriate glycemic index—this is a way of ranking foods containing carbohydrate according to their effect on blood glucose levels. If you have diabetes, combining foods with a low glycemic index with main meals can help to control blood glucose levels.

Diet makes all the difference to the long-term health of someone with diabetes. If you have diabetes you should reduce your intake of fat, particularly saturated or animal fat, base your meals and snacks on carbohydrate foods like bread and pasta, and also eat plenty of fruit and vegetables. Salt and sugar should be used in only minimal amounts.

Eating for good health is about matching your intake of food to your body's needs and keeping your weight at a healthy level. It is also about understanding how to balance food choices, so that you can enjoy eating without feeling guilty. Even high-fat, high-sugar foods can be incorporated into your diet plan, if you know how.

What is diabetes?

Diabetes is a common condition in which the glucose (sugar) level in the blood is too high. Normally, the level of glucose in the blood is controlled by a hormone called insulin, which is produced by the pancreas. Insulin enables the glucose to enter various cells in the body, where it is used to fuel the body's energy requirements. In the case of someone with diabetes, the body doesn't produce any or enough insulin to regulate the glucose, or the insulin that it does produce does not do the job properly. As a result, the glucose is unable to get into the cells where it is required to provide energy and instead remains in the bloodstream at high levels. Glucose comes from the digestion of starchy foods such as bread and pasta, from sugar and other sweet foods, and it is also made in the liver.

Diabetes is a genetic condition, which means that it tends to run in families. In addition, scientists are uncertain as to whether any environmental factors may also play a part in the development of diabetes.

The number of cases of diabetes is increasing. It is currently estimated that 150 million people worldwide suffer from diabetes.

It is currently estimated that 150 million of the world's population have diabetes. This is expected to rise to 300 million by the year 2025. Diabetes is more common among certain ethnic groups, particularly Asian and African-Caribbean populations. Almost 6 percent of people in the US (nearly 16 million people) have diabetes, of whom 5 million are unaware that they have it. In the UK, about 3 percent of people are known to have diabetes (about 1.4 million people) and for every person diagnosed with diabetes, there is probably another person who does not know they have the condition. Although diabetes can occur at any age, it is rare in young children and becomes more common as people get older.

The main symptoms of untreated diabetes are increased thirst, frequently passing large amounts of urine, extreme tiredness, weight loss, genital itching, and blurred vision.

Managing your diabetes
Managing your diabetes is simply about everyday control—keeping your blood glucose levels as close to normal as you can, while still

The main types of diabetes

There are two main types of diabetes: *Type 1* and *Type 2*.

• **Type 1**, or insulin dependent, diabetes develops when the body stops producing insulin because the cells in the pancreas that make it have been destroyed. It usually appears before the age of 40 and is treated by insulin injections and diet.

• **Type 2** diabetes, or non insulin dependent diabetes, is the most common type of diabetes. It develops when the body can still produce insulin, but not enough for its needs, or when the insulin that it does produce does not work properly. It usually appears in people over the age of 40 and may be treated by diet alone, or by diet in conjunction with tablets or insulin injections. People who are overweight are more likely to develop Type 2 diabetes and at least 80 percent of people diagnosed with Type 2 diabetes have a weight problem.

maintaining a normal lifestyle. Blood glucose levels are measured in millimols per liter of blood, and your doctor or diabetes nurse will be able to advise you on the levels that are best for you.

Essentially, blood glucose levels can be controlled by sticking to sensible eating habits and choosing the best foods for your body's system, together with following a healthy lifestyle that involves exercise and not smoking. These factors, in conjunction with diabetes medication if necessary, will help to protect against the long-term complications of diabetes. These can include damage to the eyes, kidneys, nerves, heart, and major arteries.

Managing your weight

What you eat directly affects your weight and your blood glucose levels. It can also influence the amount of fat in your blood. If you are overweight, losing weight will help you control your diabetes. Talk to your doctor if you are not sure how much you need to lose or how to lose it. You should also discuss any dietary changes, as you may need to adjust your medication at the same time. If you are overweight, even losing just 5 pounds and keeping it off will be beneficial to your health. Losing weight:

- Helps to control blood glucose levels by reducing the body's resistance to insulin
- Helps lower blood fats like cholesterol
- Lowers blood pressure
- Reduces the risk of heart disease and stroke

If you have diabetes you should have regular check-ups with your doctor or diabetes nurse to make sure that your diabetes is under control, and to screen for any of the complications associated with diabetes.

Cutting down and being more active

It is important to monitor your diabetes carefully when making changes to your diet. Cutting down on snacks or simply choosing low-fat foods like fruit instead of cookies may be all that is required to lose weight. Or you may need to go a step further and cut down on the amount of food you normally eat at a meal, in particular cutting down on fatty foods in your diet. Eating more fruit and vegetables at meal times can help reduce your calorie intake, while still providing the volume of food you are used to eating.

Becoming more active will also help you to lose weight, as well as improve your sensitivity to insulin and your general health and fitness. Remember that making gradual lifestyle changes that you can maintain in the long term will be more successful than trying to implement sudden and radical new changes. A combination of increased exercise and fewer calories is the best way to lose weight.

Hypoglycemia

If you have diabetes it is important to keep your blood glucose levels fairly stable in order to minimize the risk of developing any of the long-term complications of diabetes (see page 9). "Hypo" (short for hypoglycemia) is a term used to describe a low blood glucose level. A hypo can be unpleasant and is more likely to happen when you are treated with insulin, but can also happen if you take certain diabetes tablets.

What causes a hypo?

However well controlled your diabetes is, you may still experience a hypo because of a late or missed meal or too little carbohydrate at a meal. Other reasons for having hypoglycemia may include having too much insulin or medication, or drinking excess alcohol or having alcohol without food. Alcohol inhibits glucose production by the liver and in this way can lower blood glucose levels. Changing medication or undertaking unusually strenuous activity without having additional carbohydrate may also trigger a hypo, because exercise also lowers blood glucose levels.

Treating a hypo

If you identify the symptoms of a hypo (see box, top right), take some form of sugar immediately in order to make sure your blood glucose level rises and returns to normal. Sugar in the form of a sugary soft drink or four or five glucose candies should provide enough to treat the symptoms, but it is important to make sure that your blood glucose levels get back to normal before you do anything else. You should also have a meal or snack containing some sort of carbohydrate food, such as bread, pasta, or cereal, immediately after you have treated your hypo, to ensure that your glucose level is safe.

Hypo symptoms

The most common symptoms of hypoglycemia are:
- Sweating
- Trembling
- Feeling hungry
- Anxiety and irritability
- Fast pulse and palpitations
- Blurred vision
- Tingling lips
- Going pale

Nutrition and diabetes

As more and more information is collected from research into diabetes, the dietary guidelines for people with diabetes have tended to change in emphasis. If you are diagnosed with diabetes, you should aim to shift the balance of your diet (see the guidelines, opposite) so as to control your blood glucose levels and help you manage your condition more easily. However, you should consider the guidelines as goals that you move toward rather than rigid targets. Start by assessing your current eating habits and consider any changes that you need to make to your usual diet, your food choices, or meal planning in the context of a framework, rather than as a set of rules that can never be broken. Establishing long-term healthy eating habits can also help you reach personal targets such as your ideal weight and good cholesterol and blood pressure levels. The goals you set for yourself do not have to seem impossible. They can be as simple and straightforward as eating a piece of fruit instead of a cookie as a snack, adding salad or vegetables to your main meal, or using pasta or legumes a couple of times a week. The main areas to consider are reducing fat and salt intake, eating more starchy carbohydrate foods, as well as fruits, vegetables, and legumes, and enjoying a good variety of foods—and recipes.

In the past, a restricted carbohydrate diet and, in particular, a restricted sugar intake was considered the best way to control diabetes. As a result, many people still believe that if you have diabetes you have to stick to a rigid diet and cut out foods such as cakes and desserts. This is not the case at all and, whatever your individual dietary needs, the meals you make for yourself can be quite delicious and just as suitable for all your family and friends as well. In the same way, you don't have to miss out on special occasions—it is simply more important to get it right most of the time.

It is not necessarily the case that if you have diabetes you have to stick to a rigid diet and cut out foods such as cakes and puddings. You should still be able to enjoy a wide variety of different foods as part of a balanced diet.

Anyone diagnosed with diabetes should see a Registered Dietitian through their doctor or hospital. A dietitian will provide specific dietary advice and help you work out individual targets based on your particular needs and lifestyle, enabling you to feel more in control of your diabetes.

Healthy eating guidelines for people with diabetes

Weight management
This is an essential aspect of diabetes care. Being overweight makes it more difficult for you to control your blood glucose levels, your blood cholesterol levels, and your blood pressure. So, it is important to try to get to the weight that is right for you and retain it. If you need to lose weight, aim for a gradual weight loss that you can maintain in the long term.

Have regular meals
Eat regularly throughout the day and base your meals on starchy carbohydrate foods such as bread, potatoes, rice, pasta, and cereals. If your weight is at a healthy level, this will also help to keep your blood glucose levels stable and within a reasonable range. Go a step further and choose or incorporate carbohydrate foods with a low glycemic index (see page 15). These include pasta, rye bread, wholegrain cereals, fruits, and legumes.

Cut down on saturated fat
Eat fewer foods that are rich in saturated fat, such as fatty meats, butter, cheese, cream, and full-fat dairy foods (whole milk). Instead of butter, choose reduced- or low-fat spreads high in unsaturated fat (olive oil, canola oil, and sunflower oil), opt for light sour cream instead of heavy cream and use skim or low-fat milk.

Cut down on salt
Try not to add salt to your food—use subtle flavorings such as herbs and spices instead. Look for reduced-sodium (salt) foods when buying bread and canned foods, and avoid too many salted snacks such as chips and nuts.

Eat more fruit, vegetables, and legumes
You should aim to eat five portions of fruit, vegetables, and legumes every day. This will help to lower the glycemic index of your diet, as well as balance your meals and provide you with a source of antioxidant vitamins and minerals. It will also help you to shift the balance of what you eat, if you are trying to lose weight. Eat the same volume of food each day as you do now, but a greater proportion of fruit and vegetables, and you will end up eating a much healthier diet.

Limit your intake of sugary foods
Avoid candy, chocolate, and sugary drinks. Your diet does not have to be sugar free, but restrict your intake of sugar, fat, and calories if you are trying to lose weight.

Keep to safe drinking limits
This means a maximum of two units per day for women and three units per day for men. One unit is the equivalent of one glass of wine (5 fl oz), one shot of a spirit (1.5 fl oz), and one small beer (12 fl oz). Never drink on an empty stomach as alcohol can bring on a "hypo" (see page 11) if you are on insulin injections or certain tablets.

The glycemic index

All carbohydrate foods, when digested, are reduced to glucose, but at different rates and in varying amounts depending on the specific food. The glycemic index (GI) is a way of ranking carbohydrate foods by the effects these foods have on blood glucose levels. It is a useful way to help you to manage your carbohydrate intake and control your diabetes.

Foods are rated with a glycemic index of between 0 and 100, based on their effect on blood glucose levels when compared with pure glucose, which scores 100 on the index as it requires no digestion and is absorbed rapidly into the blood. Foods with a high GI make blood sugar levels rise quickly soon after they are eaten, whereas foods with a lower GI release glucose into the blood much more slowly.

The idea of ranking foods this way can be a useful guide to help you understand more about choosing the right carbohydrate foods to eat for the right occasion. It can also help you to maintain good blood glucose levels more easily.

If you have diabetes, you may be taking tablets or having insulin injections, or both, but whatever your situation, a healthy diet will help to manage the condition more easily. Choosing low GI foods can help you to maintain your blood glucose levels within a reasonable range, minimizing fluctuations. There is also research that shows that people who have an overall lower glycemic diet have healthier blood fat levels and a lower risk of heart disease into the bargain.

Starchy versus sugary foods

Carbohydrate foods are classed as either sugars or starchy foods. It used to be thought that all sugars were absorbed quickly into the bloodstream and starches were absorbed slowly. As a result, sugars and sugary foods were forbidden for people with diabetes. However, the measurement of glycemic indices has shown that this is not the case, and that in fact some starchy foods are absorbed just as quickly as some sugary foods. A number of different factors influence the glycemic effect of a food, including the structure of the food itself (liquids usually have a higher GI than solids, for example), and the amount of fat, protein, and fiber that a food contains.

Glycemic index values of typical foods

LOW

The following foods have a low glycemic index:

Dried lentils, boiled	30
Fettucini, cooked	32
Apples, fresh	38
Pumpernickel bread	41
Oatmeal (made with water)	42
Green grapes	46
Sweet potato, peeled and boiled	54
Bananas, fresh	55
Corn	55

MEDIUM

The following foods have a medium glycemic index:

White basmati rice, cooked	58
Honey	58
Ice cream, full-fat	61
New potatoes, peeled and boiled	62
Whole-wheat bread	69

HIGH

The following foods have a high glycemic index:

White bread	70
Mashed potato	70
Cornflakes	84
White rice, cooked	87

Food preparation and the glycemic index

The way you prepare food is also significant. In general, raw food has a lower glycemic index than cooked food. However, some canned fruits have a lower GI than the raw version, for instance peaches, apricots, and pears. Mashed or pureed foods have a higher GI than foods with a more rough-cut texture as they are digested more quickly. Likewise, smaller particles of food, for example ground cereals and flour, tend to have a higher GI than non-ground foods and whole wheat.

In the past all sugary foods were forbidden for people with diabetes. GI measurements have now shown that some starchy foods are in fact absorbed just as quickly as some sugary foods.

Selecting food for its glycemic index

Applying the glycemic index to your food selection is not about cutting out foods with a high GI, but about balancing meals. On the whole, it may be preferable to choose low GI foods but there may be times when high GI foods are a better choice, for example in treating low blood glucose levels (see page 11). It may also be preferable to choose higher GI foods when you are ill or when you are planning to undertake high-impact physical activity.

In order to reduce the overall glycemic index of your diet, you can incorporate more starchy carbohydrate foods with a low GI, such as bulgar wheat, pearl barley, pasta (white or whole-wheat), rye bread, pumpernickel, basmati rice, sweet potato, oats, legumes, and lentils. In baking, you can reduce the amount of flour and use more oat bran or rolled oats. Or you can combine foods or dishes with a lower GI, such as vegetables, fruit, and legumes, with foods or dishes that have a higher GI, to reduce the overall effect on blood glucose levels.

Applying the glycemic index to your food selection is not about cutting out foods with a high glycemic index, but about balancing meals.

Recommended dietary changes for someone with diabetes

	Sample day's eating	Recommended food if you have diabetes
Breakfast	Toast	Have oatmeal or a bran cereal AND add fruit and low-fat milk
Morning snack	Cookies	Replace with fresh fruit
Lunch	Whole-wheat bread sandwich	Use pumpernickel bread or a multigrain bread
Afternoon snack	Potato chips	Replace with fresh fruit
Evening meal	Chicken casserole with potatoes	Add lentils, cooked beans, or pearl barley. Serve with pasta or noodles

A balancing act

It is important to remember that the glycemic index is measured for individual foods, but we tend to eat combinations of foods. Combining foods with a lower GI (fruit, vegetables, and legumes) with foods that have a higher GI helps you to achieve easier blood glucose control. Low GI foods can also help you to control your appetite by making you feel fuller for longer—with the result that you eat less.

It is important not to worry about every single meal that you eat. Try to eat lower GI foods on a regular basis if you can, but don't lose sleep over it. Remember it's not about cutting out high GI foods altogether. Some combinations of foods are just meant for each other—in terms of both taste and nutrition—whatever the glycemic effects when combined. You may find that simply eating more fruit and vegetables makes a difference to your blood glucose control and your general health and wellbeing.

The recipes in this book have all been given a GI rating—low (below 55), medium (55–70), or high (over 70)—for your convenience, but you can apply the concept of glycemic indices to your meal planning in a number of ways:

1   Combine foods of a lower glycemic index (fruit, vegetables, and legumes) with foods with a higher GI

2   Choose carbohydrate foods with a low GI as the accompaniment to your meal, for example pasta rather than potatoes with meat, fish, and vegetables

3   Select a different low GI food to eat at each meal, for example eat oats at breakfast, rye bread at lunch, and pasta or legumes at supper time

Food checklist

Choose wholegrain varieties of pasta, rice, bread, and cereals as they are higher in fiber

Eat lots of fruit and vegetables—fresh, frozen, dried, or canned (five portions a day)

Use lower-fat dairy products to reduce animal fat or saturated fat intake

Choose lean cuts of meat, and always remove skin from poultry

Eat more fish

Use foods high in monounsaturated and polyunsaturated fat, and cut down on saturated fat

Avoid sugary drinks

Living with diabetes

If you have diabetes, you will inevitably have to make some changes to your way of life. However, simply by giving more careful consideration to your diet in terms of food choice, food shopping, cooking, and eating, you should be able to continue with your normal activities. Having diabetes does not mean going without life's pleasures; it just means adhering to the principles of a healthy diet that everyone should already be following and monitoring your condition with the help of healthcare professionals.

Healthy cooking

Try to incorporate the dietary guidelines on page 13, and balance the proportions of different foods in your diet in favor of fruit and vegetables and starchy foods. You can easily adapt favorite recipes to be lower in fat (see below) and salt, and balance simple meals by serving them with extra foods such as bread, salad, or vegetables.

Reducing your fat intake

There are a number of ways you can cut down on fat in cooking:

• Broil, bake, poach, steam, dry roast, or dry fry foods rather than fry them in oil

• Use a low-fat spread or low-fat cheese spread in place of full-fat butter or margarine

• Make a paste with flour and liquid to thicken sauces, rather than using flour and butter to make a traditional roux-based sauce

• Use lean cuts of meat and poultry and remove visible fat and skin before cooking

• Skim off fat after cooking

• Eat more meat alternatives such as legumes, quorn, tofu, and textured-vegetable-protein products

• Use more starchy carbohydrate foods such as bulgar wheat, pasta, rice, and other cereals as a basis for main meals

Get into the habit of using the right sort of fat

1   Use oils and spreads that are high in monounsaturated fats (olive oil, canola oil, and nut oils) or polyunsaturated fats (sunflower, safflower, soy, corn, or grapeseed oils)

2   Look out for unsalted versions of spreads and fats to reduce your sodium intake

Top 10 shopping tips

1 Choose low-fat dairy products, such as skim or low-fat milk, low-fat yogurts, and low- or reduced-fat spreads instead of butter. Use light sour cream or yogurt in place of cream

2 Buy lean meat and poultry

3 Buy canned fish to keep in your pantry

4 Stock up with a range of cooking oils, such as sesame, walnut, and olive, and a good range of spices and dried, bottled, or frozen herbs

5 Mustard, flavored vinegars, balsamic vinegar, soy sauce, Thai fish sauce, Worcestershire sauce, and Tabasco are also useful pantry items

6 Look out for alternative seasonings such as seaweed salt and sea salt. Although these products still contain as much sodium, you use less. Also look for reduced-sodium bouillon cubes

7 Use fat-free or low-calorie dressings for quick and easy flavorings, but watch the sodium content

8 Cereals like rolled oats, rice, pasta, pearl barley, bulgar wheat, and dried beans and legumes can form the basis of a hearty meal

9 Canned tomatoes and corn supplement the vegetables in a meal

10 Canned fruits and dried fruits are also useful reserves

Healthy eating is easily achievable. All it means is that you must give more careful consideration to your diet, food shopping, cooking, and lifestyle.

Understanding food labels

Food labels provide information about the nutritional content of food. When comparing food labels, you need to consider how the food will fit into your overall diet—how much of it you are likely to eat and how often, and whether it is a good choice in terms of calorie, fat, and carbohydrate content. You may feel that certain foods are high in fat and calories, and therefore not a good choice on an everyday basis, but those foods you can save for occasional treats. The example below shows how to read a food label and get the information you need.

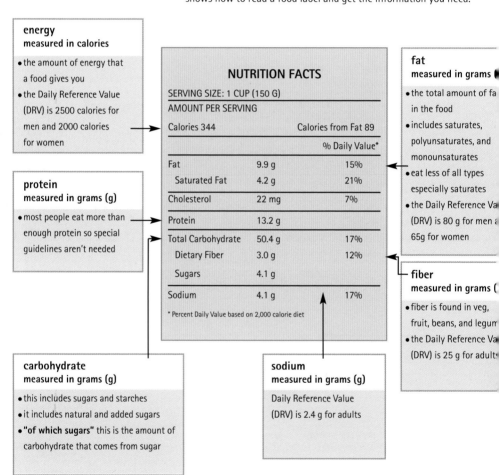

energy
measured in calories

• the amount of energy that a food gives you
• the Daily Reference Value (DRV) is 2500 calories for men and 2000 calories for women

protein
measured in grams (g)

• most people eat more than enough protein so special guidelines aren't needed

NUTRITION FACTS

SERVING SIZE: 1 CUP (150 G)

AMOUNT PER SERVING

Calories 344		Calories from Fat 89
		% Daily Value*
Fat	9.9 g	15%
Saturated Fat	4.2 g	21%
Cholesterol	22 mg	7%
Protein	13.2 g	
Total Carbohydrate	50.4 g	17%
Dietary Fiber	3.0 g	12%
Sugars	4.1 g	
Sodium	4.1 g	17%

* Percent Daily Value based on 2,000 calorie diet

fat
measured in grams

• the total amount of fa in the food
• includes saturates, polyunsaturates, and monounsaturates
• eat less of all types especially saturates
• the Daily Reference Va (DRV) is 80 g for men a 65g for women

fiber
measured in grams

• fiber is found in veg, fruit, beans, and legum
• the Daily Reference Va (DRV) is 25 g for adult

carbohydrate
measured in grams (g)

• this includes sugars and starches
• it includes natural and added sugars
• "of which sugars" this is the amount of carbohydrate that comes from sugar

sodium
measured in grams (g)

Daily Reference Value (DRV) is 2.4 g for adults

Eating out

Having diabetes does not mean that you can't enjoy meals out with friends and family. It does, however, mean that you need to take more care with meal planning and monitoring your diabetes. You may need to seek advice from your doctor or diabetes nurse if you are going to be eating at an unusual time of day and your medication needs adjustment. If your diabetes is treated with diet alone, or a combination of diet and tablets, the timing will not be so crucial. If you have insulin injections, however, you need to ensure that your meal will not be delayed.

Simple self-help measures

Simple measures, such as having a small snack like a banana before you go out, or delaying your injection until you arrive at the restaurant or party, may be all that is needed. You can always ask for some bread to nibble if you are a little behind your normal schedule. Never drink alcohol on an empty stomach because alcohol lowers your blood glucose level and you therefore risk hypoglycemia (see page 11). As a general rule, drink alcohol with food rather than before a meal or before food is served.

If you eat out only rarely, you should be able to enjoy a special occasion and not worry too much about the additional calories or fat—as long as your blood glucose level is under control.

Eating out regularly

If you eat out regularly, then you need to choose your food more carefully. Try to stick to one or two courses rather than a full menu all the time, and avoid high-fat foods such as pies, creamy sauces and soups, fried foods and french fries. Make sure you have plenty of vegetables, salad, and carbohydrate-based dishes. Pasta or rice with legumes, tomato- and vegetable-based sauces are very good choices. Avoid eating heavy desserts laden with cream on a regular basis.

Having diabetes does not mean that you cannot enjoy special celebrations or the occasional meal out.

The recipes

Rice, pasta, and other grains
You can create complete meals in no time at all by using different combinations of vegetables, meat, and fish with starchy carbohydrate foods such as rice, pasta, and grains.

Beans, seeds, and legumes
Peas, beans, and lentils all have a low glycemic index of less than 50. They are high in protein and fiber and low in fat, and can be used to lower the glycemic index of everyone's diet.

Eat more potatoes
Although potatoes have a higher glycemic index than other starchy staples such as pasta, they combine well with other foods, including eggs and cheese, and vegetables or legumes, to make quick recipes that are filling and well balanced.

Extra fruit and vegetables
By replacing a proportion of your meal with fruit and vegetables, you can automatically reduce the calories, increase the fiber content, and lower the glycemic index. You also increase your vitamin and mineral intake and reduce your salt intake.

Bread as a basis
Bread is a staple that can be used to accompany main meals or form the basis for light meals at all times of the day. There are many different kinds of breads, including those made from different cereal grains, such as wheat, rye, and oats.

Rice, pasta, and other grains

Pasta with shrimp, peas, and mint

1 Cook the pasta according to package instructions, adding the peas 2 minutes before the end of cooking time. Drain.

2 Meanwhile, heat the oil in a nonstick saucepan, add the onion and garlic, and fry for 2–3 minutes until they begin to soften.

3 Add the wine to the pan, bring to a boil and boil until reduced by about a half.

4 Stir in the shrimp, sour cream, Parmesan, and mint and heat through. Season to taste with salt and pepper. Toss the sauce through the pasta and serve garnished with mint leaves.

Preparation time 10 minutes
Cooking time 12 minutes

12 oz dried pasta shapes
1 ⅓ cups frozen peas
1 tablespoon olive oil
1 onion, sliced
1 garlic clove, crushed
⅔ cup dry white wine
7 oz cooked jumbo shrimp
6 tablespoons light sour cream
2 tablespoons freshly grated Parmesan cheese
2 tablespoons chopped mint
salt and pepper
mint leaves, to garnish

Nutritional tip
Shellfish are a source of cholesterol; however they can be included in your diet as blood cholesterol is more affected by the amount of saturated fat in a diet and other factors such as weight.

Nutritional facts
- GI rating – Low
- Calories – 444
- Protein – 25 g
- Carbohydrate – 75 g
- Fat – 11 g

Pork balls with tomato sauce and Spaghetti

Preparation time 10 minutes
Cooking time 20 minutes

12 oz dried spaghetti
10 oz ground pork
1 onion, finely chopped
1 garlic clove, crushed
$\frac{1}{2}$ teaspoon paprika
2 teaspoons tomato paste
3 cups passata (sieved tomatoes)
salt and pepper

1 Cook the spaghetti according to package instructions.

2 Meanwhile, mix together the pork, onion, garlic, and paprika and season with salt and pepper. Shape the mixture into 12 balls.

3 Place the meatballs on a broiler pan and cook under a preheated broiler for 6–7 minutes, turning occasionally, until browned and cooked through.

4 Drain the spaghetti, return it to the saucepan, and stir in the tomato paste, passata, and the meatballs. Season to taste with salt and pepper, heat through, and serve.

Nutritional tip
Dry roast meatballs rather than frying them so that you reduce your intake of fat.

Nutritional facts
- GI rating – Low
- Calories – 486
- Protein – 27 g
- Carbohydrate – 78 g
- Fat – 9 g

Pasta with tomato, spinach, and ricotta sauce ⓥ

Preparation time 10 minutes
Cooking time 15 minutes

12 oz dried pasta shapes
1 teaspoon olive oil
1 garlic clove, crushed
1 onion, sliced
$\frac{1}{2}$ teaspoon dried red pepper flakes
3 cups passata (sieved tomatoes)
4 cups baby spinach leaves
$\frac{2}{3}$ cup ricotta cheese
salt and pepper

1 Cook the pasta according to package instructions and drain.

2 Meanwhile, heat the oil in a saucepan, add the garlic and onion and fry for 3–4 minutes. Add the pepper flakes and continue to fry for 1 minute.

3 Stir in the passata and simmer for 2 minutes. Add the spinach and ricotta, stir until the spinach has wilted then simmer for 3–4 minutes.

4 Toss the pasta through the sauce, season to taste with salt and pepper, and serve.

Nutritional tip
Ricotta is a soft cheese which can be used in sauces. It has a low to medium fat content.

Nutritional facts
- GI rating – Low
- Calories – 432
- Protein – 18 g
- Carbohydrate – 79 g
- Fat – 7 g

Herbed pasta with roasted cherry tomatoes ⓥ

Preparation time 10 minutes
Cooking time 15 minutes

12 oz dried pasta shapes

15 cherry tomatoes, halved

2 tablespoons pesto

1 tablespoon white wine vinegar

2 tablespoons capers, drained

2 anchovy fillets, chopped (optional)

2 tablespoons chopped mixed herbs (such as parsley and basil)

salt and pepper

Parmesan cheese shavings, to garnish

crisp green salad, to serve

1 Cook the pasta according to package instructions and drain.

2 Meanwhile, place the tomatoes under a preheated hot broiler and cook for about 15 minutes until they are slightly charred and beginning to dry out.

3 Place the pesto, vinegar, capers, anchovies, and herbs in a food processor or blender and blend until almost smooth but retaining a little texture.

4 Toss the sauce through the hot pasta with the tomatoes, season to taste with salt and pepper, and serve with some Parmesan shavings and a crisp green salad.

Nutritional tip
Pasta is a good staple for use in vegetarian meals as it is also a source of protein.

Nutritional facts
- GI rating – Low
- Calories – 406
- Protein – 15 g
- Carbohydrate – 72 g
- Fat – 7 g

Nutty citrus wild rice salad (V)

Preparation time 10 minutes
Cooking time 15 minutes

1 cup mixed long-grain and wild rice

1 tablespoon wholegrain mustard

grated zest and juice of 1 large orange

1 orange, segmented

4 scallions, sliced

12 cherry tomatoes, quartered

$^{1}/_{2}$ cup mixed seeds (such as pumpkin, sunflower, and pine nuts), toasted

2 oz feta cheese, crumbled

1$^{1}/_{4}$ cups watercress, chopped

2 tablespoons chopped parsley

salt and pepper

1 Cook the rice according to package instructions. Drain, then refresh under cold running water.

2 Mix together the mustard and the orange zest and juice. Stir through the rice then add the orange segments, scallions, tomatoes, mixed seeds, feta, watercress, and parsley. Season to taste with salt and pepper and serve.

Nutritional tip
Feta cheese has a high water content and a high sodium content. It is particularly good in salads, but should be used sparingly.

Nutritional facts
- GI rating – Low
- Calories – 316
- Protein – 10 g
- Carbohydrate – 50 g
- Fat – 9 g

Thai chicken curry with citrus rice

Preparation time 15 minutes
Cooking time 20 minutes

1 tablespoon sunflower oil
1 lemon grass stalk, cut into 4
2 kaffir lime leaves, halved
1–2 red chilies, finely chopped
1 inch piece of fresh ginger root, peeled and grated
1 onion, finely chopped
1 garlic clove, crushed
1 red bell pepper, cored, seeded, and chopped
1 green bell pepper, cored, seeded, and chopped
3 boneless, skinless chicken breasts, chopped
1 ½ cups can reduced-fat coconut milk
²⁄₃ cup chicken stock
4 tablespoons chopped cilantro leaves
1 ¼ cups basmati rice
grated zest and juice of 2 limes
salt and pepper

1 Heat the oil in a pan and add the lemon grass, lime leaves, chili, ginger, onion, and garlic, and fry for 2 minutes.

2 Add the bell peppers and chicken and continue to fry for 5 minutes.

3 Pour in the coconut milk and the stock and simmer for an additional 10 minutes or until the chicken is cooked through.

4 Stir in half of the cilantro and season to taste with salt and pepper.

5 Meanwhile, put the rice into a pan of lightly salted boiling water with half the lime zest and juice. Cook according to package instructions until tender, then drain. Stir in the remaining lime zest and juice and cilantro. Serve with the curry.

Nutritional tip
Coconut milk is high in saturated fat and calories, so look out for the reduced-fat version and use sparingly.

Nutritional facts
● **GI rating** – Medium
● **Calories** – 451
● **Protein** – 38 g
● **Carbohydrate** – 61 g
● **Fat** – 6 g

Smoked salmon and cream cheese risotto

Preparation time 10 minutes
Cooking time 25 minutes

2 teaspoons olive oil

1 onion, finely chopped

2 garlic cloves, crushed

1 $\frac{1}{2}$ cups risotto rice

$\frac{2}{3}$ cup dry white wine

3 $\frac{3}{4}$ cups simmering vegetable stock

$\frac{1}{2}$ cup light cream cheese

4 oz smoked salmon, chopped

4 tablespoons chopped herbs (such as chives, parsley, or dill weed)

salt and pepper

1 Heat the oil in a large saucepan, add the onion and garlic and fry for 2–3 minutes until they begin to soften.

2 Stir in the rice and continue to cook for 1 minute. Add the wine and cook, stirring, until all the wine has been absorbed.

3 Reduce the heat and add the stock a little at a time, stirring continuously, and allowing each amount of stock to be absorbed before adding the next. Continue until all the stock has been absorbed.

4 Stir in the cream cheese, smoked salmon, and herbs, season to taste with salt and pepper, and serve.

Nutritional tip

Smoked salmon is an oily fish which contains omega-3 fatty acids, which help to protect against heart disease. Try to eat oily fish at least once a week.

Nutritional facts

- GI rating – Medium
- Calories – 428
- Protein – 17 g
- Carbohydrate – 60 g
- Fat – 8 g

Mixed mushroom risotto Ⓥ

Preparation time 10 minutes
Cooking time 20 minutes

²/₃ cup dried porcini mushrooms
1 tablespoon olive oil
1 onion, finely chopped
2 garlic cloves, crushed
1½ cups risotto rice
²/₃ cup dry white wine
3¾ cups simmering vegetable stock
1 lb mixed mushrooms (such as flat cap, button, and brown)
handful of chopped parsley
¼ cup grated Parmesan cheese
salt and pepper

1 Place the dried mushrooms in a bowl, cover with a cup of boiling water and set aside.

2 Heat a little of the oil in a large skillet, add the onion and garlic and fry for 2–3 minutes until beginning to soften.

3 Add the rice and continue to cook for 1 minute, stirring to coat the rice in the oil. Add the wine and cook, stirring, until it has been absorbed.

4 Reduce the heat and add the stock a little at a time, stirring continuously. Allow each amount of stock to be absorbed before adding the next. Continue until all the stock has been absorbed, then add the porcini mushrooms and their liquid.

5 Heat the remaining oil in another saucepan and fry the fresh mushrooms until cooked. Stir into the rice mixture with the parsley and Parmesan, season to taste with salt and pepper, and serve.

Nutritional tip
Parmesan cheese is a hard cheese; it is high in fat so grate finely and use sparingly.

Nutritional facts
- GI rating – Medium
- Calories – 407
- Protein – 13 g
- Carbohydrate – 60 g
- Fat – 9 g

Vegetable biryani Ⓥ

1 Cook the rice in boiling water according to package instructions. Drain well.

2 Meanwhile, heat the oil in a nonstick saucepan, add the carrots, potato, ginger, and garlic and fry for 10 minutes until they are beginning to soften.

3 Stir in the cauliflower, beans, curry paste, turmeric, and cinnamon and cook for 1 minute.

4 Stir in the yogurt and raisins. Pile the rice onto the vegetable mixture. Cover and cook over a low heat for 10 minutes, checking from time to time that it isn't sticking to the pan.

5 Turn the biryani into a large serving dish, sprinkle with the nuts and cilantro, and serve.

1¼ cups long-grain rice
1 tablespoon olive oil
2 carrots, chopped
1 large potato, chopped
1 tablespoon grated fresh ginger root
2 garlic cloves, crushed
½ cup cauliflower florets
4 oz green beans, halved
1 tablespoon hot curry paste
1 teaspoon turmeric
½ teaspoon ground cinnamon
⅔ cup plain yogurt
2 tablespoons raisins
⅓ cup cashew nuts, toasted
2 tablespoons chopped cilantro leaves

Nutritional tip
Nuts are high in fat but they are also a good source of protein and fiber in the diet.

Nutritional facts
- GI rating – Medium
- Calories – 450
- Protein – 12 g
- Carbohydrate – 72 g
- Fat – 11 g

Couscous with broiled vegetables Ⓥ

Preparation time 10 minutes
Cooking time 20 minutes

1^2/$_3$ cups couscous

2 cups boiling water

2 red bell peppers, cored, seeded, and quartered

1 orange bell pepper, cored, seeded, and quartered

6 baby zucchini, halved lengthwise

2 red onions, cut into wedges

24 cherry tomatoes

2 garlic cloves, finely sliced

2 tablespoons olive oil

4 oz asparagus spears

grated zest and juice of 1 lemon

4 tablespoons chopped herbs (such as parsley or mint)

salt and pepper

1 Tip the couscous into a large bowl, pour over the water, cover, and set aside for 10 minutes while preparing the remaining ingredients.

2 Place the peppers, zucchini, onions, tomatoes, and garlic in a broiler pan in one layer, drizzle over the oil and cook under a preheated hot broiler for 5–6 minutes, turning the vegetables occasionally.

3 Add the asparagus to the pan and continue to broil for 2–3 minutes until the vegetables are tender and lightly charred. When they are cool enough to handle, remove the skins from the peppers and discard.

4 Fork through the couscous to separate the grains. Toss with the vegetables, lime zest and juice, and herbs, season to taste with salt and pepper, and serve.

Nutritional tip
Cherry tomatoes are a good source of antioxidants in the diet. Antioxidants help to improve general health and are thought to slow down the aging process in the body.

Nutritional facts
• **GI rating** – Medium
• **Calories** – 470
• **Protein** – 12 g
• **Carbohydrate** – 85 g
• **Fat** – 8 g

Chicken tagine with fruity couscous

Preparation time 10 minutes
Cooking time 20 minutes

1 tablespoon olive oil
8 medium boneless, skinless chicken thighs
1 large onion, chopped
2 garlic cloves, crushed
1 teaspoon ground cumin
$\frac{1}{2}$ teaspoon ground ginger
1 teaspoon paprika
$\frac{2}{3}$ cup ready-to-eat dried apricots, halved
13 oz can chickpeas, drained and rinsed
$\frac{1}{4}$ teaspoon saffron threads
$1\frac{3}{4}$ cups chicken stock
grated zest and juice of $\frac{1}{2}$ lemon
$\frac{1}{2}$ cup pitted green olives
$1\frac{2}{3}$ cups couscous
$\frac{2}{3}$ cup golden raisins
2 cups boiling water
4 tablespoons chopped mint
4 tablespoons chopped flat leaf parsley
salt and pepper

1 Heat the oil in a large casserole. Add the chicken thighs, onion, and garlic and fry gently for 3–4 minutes until the chicken is beginning to brown.

2 Stir in the cumin, ginger, and paprika and fry for 1 minute. Add the apricots, chickpeas, saffron, stock, lemon zest and juice, and olives to the pan, cover, and simmer for 15 minutes.

3 Meanwhile, place the couscous in a bowl with the golden raisins and pour over the boiling water. Allow to soak for about 5 minutes until the water has been absorbed, fluffing up the grains from time to time with a fork.

4 Stir the mint into the couscous and the parsley into the chicken tagine. Season to taste with salt and pepper. Serve the tagine on top of the couscous with plenty of the cooking liquid.

Nutritional tip
This recipe can be served as a vegetarian dish without the chicken; it is just as nutritious and delicious.

Nutritional facts
- GI rating – Medium
- Calories – 544
- Protein – 35 g
- Carbohydrate – 67 g
- Fat – 15 g

Roasted tomato and bulgar wheat salad Ⓥ

Preparation time 10 minutes
Cooking time 15 minutes

1 1/4 cups bulgar wheat

20 cherry tomatoes, halved

2 red bell peppers, cored, seeded, and quartered

2 tablespoons olive oil

3 tablespoons pine nuts, toasted

13 oz can artichoke hearts, drained

2 oz feta cheese, crumbled

2 tablespoons chopped parsley

grated zest and juice of 1 lemon

1 tablespoon honey

2 teaspoons Dijon mustard

salt and pepper

1 Place the bulgar wheat in a large bowl, cover with boiling water, and allow to soak for 10–15 minutes until the grains are tender. Drain well.

2 Meanwhile, place the tomatoes and peppers on a broiler pan, drizzle with half the oil and season with salt and pepper. Place under a preheated hot broiler for 5–7 minutes, turning occasionally, until charred and tender.

3 Remove and discard the skin from the peppers, slice the flesh, and add to the bulgar wheat, along with the tomatoes, pine nuts, artichoke hearts, feta, and parsley.

4 Beat together the lemon zest and juice, honey, mustard, and the remaining oil, and drizzle over the salad. Season to taste with salt and pepper, toss to combine, and serve.

Nutritional tip
Artichokes are good sources of folate and potassium in the diet. Canned artichokes can be as nutritious as fresh ones.

Nutritional facts
- GI rating – Medium
- Calories – 380
- Protein – 11 g
- Carbohydrate – 60 g
- Fat – 11 g

Pearl barley salad with griddled chicken

Preparation time 10 minutes
Cooking time 10 minutes

1 Brush each chicken piece with a little oil. Heat a griddle until hot and cook the chicken for 4–5 minutes on each side until cooked and browned. Cut each breast into 4 slices.

2 Stir the remaining oil into the barley, and add the onion, chili, cilantro, lime zest and juice, and bell pepper. Season to taste with salt and pepper and stir to combine.

3 Serve the barley topped with the chicken, garnished with parsley and lime wedges.

4 boneless, skinless chicken breasts

1 tablespoon olive oil

$^1\!/_2$ cup pearl barley, cooked according to package instructions

1 red onion, finely chopped

1 red chili, finely chopped

4 tablespoons chopped cilantro leaves

grated zest and juice of 2 limes

1 red bell pepper, cored, seeded, and finely chopped

salt and pepper

TO GARNISH
parsley sprigs
lime wedges

Nutritional tip
Pearl barley is high in soluble fiber and can be used as a substitute for rice.

Nutritional facts
- GI rating – Low
- Calories – 274
- Protein – 27 g
- Carbohydrate – 31 g
- Fat – 5 g

Shrimp and noodle soup

Preparation time 5 minutes
Cooking time 15 minutes

1 Put the stock into a saucepan with the lime leaves and lemon grass, bring to a boil, and simmer for 10 minutes.

2 Add the noodles to the stock and cook according to package instructions. After 2 minutes, add the peas, corn, shrimp, scallions, and soy sauce. Serve in individual bowls.

3³/₄ cups vegetable or chicken stock

2 kaffir lime leaves

1 lemon grass stalk, lightly bruised

5 oz dried egg noodles

¹/₃ cup frozen peas

¹/₃ cup frozen corn

4 oz large, cooked and peeled shrimp

4 scallions, sliced

2 teaspoons soy sauce

Nutritional tip
Frozen vegetables can be just as nutritious as fresh vegetables. As well as keeping a good color and flavor, most of the nutrients are retained.

Nutritional facts
- **GI rating** – Low
- **Calories** – 187
- **Protein** – 10 g
- **Carbohydrate** – 30 g
- **Fat** – 3 g

Teriyaki salmon on noodles

Preparation time 10 minutes
Cooking time 12 minutes

4 pieces skinless salmon fillet, about 4 oz each
2 tablespoons soy sauce
1 tablespoon dry sherry
2 tablespoons brown sugar
2 garlic cloves, crushed
1 teaspoon grated fresh ginger root
1 tablespoon sesame oil
2 tablespoons water
2 tablespoons sesame seeds
2 scallions, chopped
8 oz dried rice noodles, cooked according to package instructions
3 tablespoons chopped cilantro leaves

1 Place the salmon on a foil-lined broiler pan. Mix together the soy sauce, sherry, sugar, garlic, ginger, half of the oil, and the water. Brush half of the marinade over the salmon and set aside for 10 minutes.

2 Cook the salmon under a preheated hot broiler for 5–6 minutes, turning it halfway through the cooking time and brushing with a little more of the marinade.

3 Meanwhile, heat the remaining oil in a saucepan, add the sesame seeds and scallions and fry for 1 minute.

4 Add the noodles and any remaining marinade to the saucepan and heat through. Stir in the cilantro leaves. Serve the salmon on a bed of noodles.

Nutritional tip
Sesame seeds are a source of calcium and magnesium and an excellent addition to exotic dishes.

Nutritional facts
- GI rating – Low
- Calories – 504
- Protein – 30 g
- Carbohydrate – 50 g
- Fat – 20 g

Thai beef and noodle salad

8 oz piece lean sirloin steak

1 1/2 cups bean sprouts

1 red bell pepper, cored, seeded, and finely sliced

1/2 cucumber, peeled, seeded, and sliced

1 1/4 cups arugula

7 oz dried egg noodles, cooked according to package instructions

DRESSING

grated zest and juice of 1 lime

1 tablespoon sesame oil

1 tablespoon Thai fish sauce

1 red chili, seeded and finely sliced

4 tablespoons chopped cilantro leaves

1 Heat a griddle or skillet until very hot. Add the steak and fry for 1-2 minutes on each side, depending how you prefer your meat cooked. Remove from the heat and allow to rest for about 5 minutes.

2 Toss the bean sprouts, bell pepper, cucumber, and arugula with the noodles.

3 Mix together the dressing ingredients, pour over the salad, and combine well. Divide between 4 plates.

4 Slice the steak into thin strips and place on top of the individual salads, then serve.

Nutritional tip
Lean red meat is low in fat and calories; it is also a good source of iron.

Nutritional facts
- GI rating – Low
- Calories – 317
- Protein – 18 g
- Carbohydrate – 40 g
- Fat – 10 g

Beans, seeds, and legumes

Chicken liver, black-eyed pea, and spinach salad

1 Heat the oil in a pan, add the onion and garlic and fry for 2 minutes.

2 Add the chicken livers and fry for 3–4 minutes until just cooked through.

3 Stir in the balsamic vinegar, tomatoes, and peas and heat through for an additional 2 minutes. Toss through the spinach and serve with crusty bread.

Preparation time 10 minutes
Cooking time 10 minutes

1 tablespoon olive oil
1 onion, sliced
1 garlic clove, crushed
8 oz chicken livers, halved
2 tablespoons balsamic vinegar
3 tomatoes, chopped
13 oz can black-eyed peas, drained and rinsed
4$\frac{1}{2}$ cups baby leaf spinach
crusty bread, to serve

Nutritional tip
Spinach is an excellent source of iron and used as a salad ingredient it provides maximum nutritional value.

Nutritional facts
- GI rating – Low
- Calories – 181
- Protein – 18 g
- Carbohydrate – 17 g
- Fat – 5 g

Chili bean soup with avocado salsa Ⓥ

Preparation time 5 minutes
Cooking time 25 minutes

1 tablespoon oil

1 large onion, chopped

2 garlic cloves, crushed

2 red chilies, finely chopped

1 teaspoon ground cumin

$1/2$ teaspoon ground cinnamon

2 x 13 oz cans kidney beans, drained and rinsed

13 oz can chopped tomatoes

$2 1/2$ cups vegetable stock

tortillas or flatbread, to serve

SALSA

1 small avocado, peeled and finely chopped

2 tomatoes, finely chopped

4 tablespoons chopped cilantro leaves

$1/2$ small red onion, finely chopped

salt and pepper

1 Heat the oil in a large saucepan, add the onion, garlic, and chilies and fry for 2–3 minutes until the onion begins to soften.

2 Add the spices and continue to fry for another minute. Add the kidney beans, tomatoes, and stock to the pan, bring to a boil, cover, and simmer for 15 minutes.

3 Transfer the soup to a food processor or blender and blend until smooth (it may be easier to do this in batches). Return the soup to the pan and heat through.

4 Meanwhile, mix together all the ingredients for the salsa.

5 Serve the soup topped with a spoonful of salsa, with tortillas or flatbread.

Nutritional tip
Avocados are a source of monounsaturated fatty acids.

Nutritional facts
- GI rating – Low
- Calories – 264
- Protein – 12 g
- Carbohydrate – 36 g
- Fat – 8 g

Herby bean cakes ⓥ

1 Place the beans in a food processor or blender and blend until almost smooth. Add half of the egg and blend again.

2 Stir in the scallions, herbs, and Stilton. Season to taste with salt and pepper.

3 Shape the mixture into 8 balls, then flatten them slightly with the palm of your hand. Coat the patties in flour, then dip them into the remaining egg, then in the bread crumbs, to coat them. Place on a lightly oiled baking sheet and drizzle with the oil.

4 Cook the bean cakes in a preheated oven at 400°F for 10–15 minutes until golden and piping hot. Garnish each serving with a parsley sprig and serve with a tomato and cucumber salad.

2 x 13 oz cans cannellini beans, drained and rinsed

2 eggs, beaten

1 bunch of scallions, finely chopped

4 tablespoons chopped herbs (such as sage, parsley, or thyme)

2 oz Stilton cheese, crumbled

4 tablespoons all-purpose flour

1 cup fine white bread crumbs

2 tablespoons oil

salt and pepper

4 parsley sprigs, to garnish

tomato and cucumber salad, to serve

Nutritional tip
Fresh parsley is a good source of vitamin C and iron.

Nutritional facts
● GI rating – Low
● Calories – 352
● Protein – 19 g
● Carbohydrate – 45 g
● Fat – 11 g

Mixed bean pâté ⓥ

1 Place all the ingredients in a food processor or blender and blend until almost smooth, but still retaining a little texture.

2 Season to taste with salt and pepper and serve with plenty of crusty bread and a crisp green salad.

2 x 13 oz cans mixed beans, drained and rinsed

4 tablespoons light sour cream

2 tablespoons chopped mixed herbs (such as cilantro and parsley)

1 tablespoon olive oil

2 tablespoons creamed horseradish

salt and pepper

TO SERVE
crusty bread
green salad

Nutritional tip
This quick pâté is a low-fat vegetarian alternative to high-fat meat pâtés.

Nutritional facts
- **GI rating** – Low
- **Calories** – 196
- **Protein** – 11 g
- **Carbohydrate** – 31 g
- **Fat** – 10 g

Sausage and bean casserole

Preparation time 10 minutes
Cooking time 20 minutes

1 tablespoon oil

1 onion, chopped

1 garlic clove, crushed

1 red bell pepper, cored, seeded, and chopped

4 lean pork sausages, quartered

2 x 13 oz cans mixed beans, drained and rinsed

13 oz can chopped tomatoes

$^2/_3$ cup vegetable stock

2 tablespoons tomato paste

2 tablespoons chopped parsley

salt and pepper

1 Heat the oil in a saucepan, add the onion, garlic, and bell pepper and fry for 2–3 minutes until beginning to soften.

2 Add the sausages and continue to cook for 5 minutes until browned all over.

3 Lightly crush half of the beans with the back of a fork and add to the pan with the remaining beans, tomatoes, vegetable stock, and tomato paste. Season to taste with salt and pepper. Bring to a boil and simmer for 10 minutes. Take the pan off the heat, stir in the parsley, and serve.

Nutritional tip
Add a carbohydrate such as mashed potato to make this a complete meal.

Nutritional facts
- **GI rating** – Low
- **Calories** – 342
- **Protein** – 20 g
- **Carbohydrate** – 38 g
- **Fat** – 13 g

Pan-fried lamb with spiced navy beans

Preparation time 10 minutes, plus marinating
Cooking time 12 minutes

1 Mix together the cumin, coriander, chili, and half the oil in a nonmetallic bowl. Add the lamb, coat it in the spices, and set aside for 10 minutes.

2 Heat the remaining oil in a nonstick pan, add the onion and garlic and fry for 3–4 minutes until softened.

3 Add the lamb and the marinade and fry for 2–3 minutes on each side, or until cooked to your desire.

4 Add the lemon juice, navy beans, mint, and sour cream and simmer for 1 minute until warmed through. Serve with salad leaves or fresh vegetables.

$\frac{1}{2}$ teaspoon ground cumin

$\frac{1}{2}$ teaspoon ground coriander

pinch of chili powder

1 tablespoon oil

4 lean lamb steaks

1 onion, sliced

1 garlic clove, crushed

4 tablespoons lemon juice

13 oz can navy beans, drained and rinsed

1 tablespoon chopped mint

2 tablespoons light sour cream

salad leaves or fresh vegetables, to serve

Nutritional tip
Serve this dish with an additional carbohydrate such as rice, potato, or pasta.

Nutritional facts
- GI rating – Low
- Calories – 261
- Protein – 26 g
- Carbohydrate – 16 g
- Fat – 12 g

Navy bean and tuna salad

1 Tip the beans and tuna into a bowl.

2 In another bowl, mix together the lemon zest and juice, mustard, honey, oil, and parsley and season to taste with salt and pepper. Pour the dressing over the beans and tuna, stir well, and set aside for 10 minutes to allow the flavors to develop.

3 Serve the salad on a bed of watercress with chunks of crusty bread.

Preparation time 5 minutes, plus marinating

2 x 13 oz cans navy beans, drained and rinsed
2 x 7 oz cans tuna in water, drained
grated zest and juice of 1 lemon
1 tablespoon Dijon mustard
1 teaspoon honey
2 tablespoons olive oil
2 tablespoons chopped parsley
salt and pepper

TO SERVE
1 bunch of watercress
crusty bread

Nutritional tip
Canned tuna is available packed in water, brine, or oil—choose water to limit your salt and fat intake.

Nutritional facts
- GI rating – Low
- Calories – 279
- Protein – 32 g
- Carbohydrate – 23 g
- Fat – 6 g

Baked trout with lima bean mash

Preparation time 10 minutes
Cooking time 20 minutes

4 trout, about 7 oz each
1 lemon, cut into wedges
4 parsley sprigs
1 onion, sliced
salt and pepper

LIMA BEAN MASH
2 x 13 oz cans lima beans,
    drained and rinsed
1 bay leaf
2 garlic cloves
1¼ cups vegetable stock
2 tablespoons light sour cream
1 tablespoon horseradish sauce

1 Cut 4 pieces of kitchen foil big enough to wrap around the fish. Place a trout in the center of each piece of foil with a couple of lemon wedges, a sprig of parsley, and some onion. Season with salt and pepper, then wrap to enclose the fish completely.

2 Bake in a preheated oven at 400°F for 15–20 minutes, or until cooked through.

3 Meanwhile, place the lima beans, bay leaf, garlic, and vegetable stock in a pan and simmer for 10 minutes. Drain the beans and remove the bay leaf.

4 Mash the bean mixture, sour cream, and horseradish until smooth. Season to taste with salt and pepper. Remove the fish from the parcels and serve with the mash.

Nutritional tip
For extra carbohydrate serve with bread or potatoes.

Nutritional facts
- **GI rating** – Low
- **Calories** – 379
- **Protein** – 48 g
- **Carbohydrate** – 22 g
- **Fat** – 12 g

Herby lentil salad with crisp parma ham

Preparation time 10 minutes
Cooking time 5 minutes

2 tablespoons olive oil
1 garlic clove, crushed
4 scallions, sliced
2 x 13 oz cans green lentils, drained and rinsed
2 tablespoons balsamic vinegar
3 tablespoons chopped herbs (such as parsley, oregano, or basil)
8 cherry tomatoes, halved
3 oz sliced Parma ham

1 Heat the oil in a nonstick saucepan, add the garlic and scallions and fry for 2 minutes.

2 Stir in the lentils, vinegar, herbs, and tomatoes and set aside.

3 Heat a skillet until hot, add the Parma ham and cook for 1–2 minutes, until crisp. Arrange the lentil salad on a large serving dish, place the ham on top, and serve.

Nutritional tip
Lentils are a good source of protein and iron, as well as containing isoflavones which may relieve menopausal symptoms.

Nutritional facts
- GI rating – Low
- Calories – 262
- Protein – 19 g
- Carbohydrate – 26 g
- Fat – 9 g

Channa chat (mixed bean salad) Ⓥ

Preparation time 10 minutes

1 Mix together all the ingredients in a bowl. Garnish with a sprinkling of garam masala and serve with plain yogurt, if desired.

13 oz can chickpeas, drained and rinsed

13 oz cooked new potatoes, quartered

13 oz can black-eyed peas, drained and rinsed

3 tablespoons corn kernels, defrosted if frozen

$\frac{1}{4}$ teaspoon salt

$\frac{1}{4}$ teaspoon chili powder, or to taste

$\frac{1}{2}$ green chili, seeded and chopped

$\frac{1}{4}$ teaspoon chat masala

1 tablespoon lemon juice

1 small onion, finely chopped

1 tomato, finely chopped

$\frac{1}{2}$ teaspoon garam masala, to garnish

plain yogurt, to serve (optional)

Nutritional tip
Chickpeas are high-energy legumes; they are also rich in carbohydrate and protein and low in fat.

Nutritional facts
- GI rating – Low
- Calories – 270
- Protein – 14 g
- Carbohydrate – 48 g
- Fat – 3 g

Spiced chickpeas in pitas ⓥ

Preparation time 10 minutes
Cooking time 20 minutes

1 tablespoon oil

2 onions, sliced

2 garlic cloves, crushed

2 tablespoons medium curry paste

6 tomatoes, chopped

2 x 13 oz cans chickpeas, drained and rinsed

1⅓ cups frozen peas, defrosted

2 tablespoons chopped cilantro leaves

4 pita breads

4 tablespoons thick yogurt

1 Heat the oil in a nonstick saucepan. Add the onion and garlic and fry for 4–5 minutes, until softened.

2 Stir in the curry paste and continue to fry for 1 minute. Add the tomatoes and chickpeas and simmer for 10 minutes.

3 Add the peas and cilantro and simmer for another minute.

4 Warm the pitas under a hot broiler and serve stuffed with the chickpea mixture and the yogurt.

Nutritional tip
Tomatoes are very good for you; they are rich in lycopene, which is a potent antioxidant thought to help protect against some forms of cancer.

Nutritional facts
- GI rating – Low
- Calories – 524
- Protein – 24 g
- Carbohydrate – 79 g
- Fat – 15 g

Mini falafel salad Ⓥ

Preparation time 15 minutes
Cooking time 5 minutes

1 Place two-thirds of the chickpeas in a food processor or blender with the ground coriander, cumin, and garlic and blend until almost smooth. Stir in the cilantro leaves and the egg yolk.

2 Form the mixture into 16 small balls and brush with the oil. Place under a preheated hot broiler and broil for 3–4 minutes until golden.

3 Divide the lettuce, cucumber, the remaining chickpeas, and the falafel between 4 plates.

4 Mix together the dressing ingredients. Serve the falafel salad with the dressing and the pita breads.

2 x 13 oz cans chickpeas, drained and rinsed

2 teaspoons ground coriander

2 teaspoons ground cumin

2 garlic cloves, crushed

2 tablespoons chopped cilantro leaves

1 egg yolk, beaten

2 tablespoons oil

toasted mini pita breads, to serve

SALAD

3 small crisphead lettuces, torn into bite-size pieces

½ cucumber, sliced

DRESSING

1¼ cups plain yogurt

3 tablespoons chopped mint

3 tablespoons chopped parsley

salt and pepper

Nutritional tip
Falafel are generally fried in oil; these mini falafel are lower in fat as they are brushed with oil and baked. Serve with the yogurt dressing, which is low in fat, high in protein, and rich in vitamins.

Nutritional facts
- GI rating – Low
- Calories – 285
- Protein – 15 g
- Carbohydrate – 31 g
- Fat – 11 g

Moroccan tomato and chickpea salad Ⓥ

Preparation time 10 minutes, plus standing

1 Mix together all the ingredients in a large nonmetallic bowl. Set aside for 10 minutes to allow the flavors to infuse, then serve.

1 red onion, finely sliced

2 x 13 oz cans chickpeas, drained and rinsed

4 tomatoes, chopped

4 tablespoons lemon juice

1 tablespoon olive oil

handful of herbs (such as mint and parsley), chopped

pinch of paprika

pinch of ground cumin

salt and pepper

Nutritional tip
Red onions are a good source of flavonols which act as antioxidants.

Nutritional facts
- GI rating – Low
- Calories – 200
- Protein – 12 g
- Carbohydrate – 30 g
- Fat – 5 g

Eat more potatoes

All-day breakfast

Preparation time 10 minutes
Cooking time 12 minutes

4 Canadian bacon slices, halved lengthwise
4 good-quality sausages, halved lengthwise
13 oz new potatoes, cooked and halved
16 mushrooms, sliced
4 tomatoes, halved
4 eggs
pepper
crusty wholegrain bread, to serve

1 Heat a large nonstick skillet and add the bacon and sausages. Fry for 2–3 minutes.

2 Add the potatoes and continue to fry for 3–4 minutes until beginning to brown. Add the mushrooms and tomatoes and continue to fry for 1–2 minutes. Drain off any excess fat and spread out all the ingredients in the pan.

3 Crack the eggs into the pan and allow to run across the base of the pan. (If your pan is not big enough, then you could cook this in two batches.)

4 Cook for another minute or until the eggs are done to your desire. Season to taste with pepper and serve with chunks of crusty wholegrain bread.

Nutritional tip
Avoid adding any oil to the pan to minimize the amount of fat in this recipe.

Nutritional facts
- **GI rating** – Low-Medium
- **Calories** – 324
- **Protein** – 20 g
- **Carbohydrate** – 21 g
- **Fat** – 15 g

Leek and potato soup Ⓥ

Preparation time 10 minutes
Cooking time 25 minutes

1 tablespoon olive oil
1 onion, chopped
1 lb leeks, finely sliced
1 lb potatoes, chopped
4 cups vegetable stock
2 tablespoons light sour cream
$1/4$ teaspoon grated nutmeg
salt and pepper

1 Heat the oil in a saucepan, add the onion and fry for 2–3 minutes. Add the leeks and potatoes and cook for 5 minutes.

2 Add the stock, bring to a boil, and simmer for 15 minutes, until the potatoes are tender.

3 Transfer to a food processor or blender and blend until smooth. Stir in the sour cream and nutmeg and season to taste with salt and plenty of black pepper.

Nutritional tip
Leeks and other members of the onion family are a good source of sulfur-containing phytochemicals, which help to protect against heart disease.

Nutritional facts
- GI rating – Medium-High
- Calories – 159
- Protein – 5 g
- Carbohydrate – 28 g
- Fat – 5 g

Scallion and potato pasties ⓥ

Preparation time 10 minutes
Cooking time 20–25 minutes

12 oz ready-made shortcrust pastry
all-purpose flour, for dusting
a little milk, for brushing

FILLING

1 medium potato, cut into small cubes

4 scallions, sliced

4 tablespoons corn kernels, defrosted if frozen

2 tablespoons light sour cream

salt and pepper

1 Roll out the pastry on a lightly floured work surface to a thickness of ⅛ inch. Using a saucer, cut out 12 rounds of pastry, 5 inches in diameter.

2 Cook the potatoes in a pan of boiling water for 5 minutes, then drain. Mix with the scallions, corn, and sour cream and season to taste with salt and pepper. Place a little of the mixture to one side of the center of each piece of pastry.

3 Dampen the edges of the pastry with a little water and fold in half to cover the filling.

4 Press down the edges with a fork, then place on a greased baking sheet. Brush with a little milk, then cook in a preheated oven at 400°F for 15–20 minutes until golden brown.

Nutritional tip
Pastry is high in fat, so roll it out thinly and use a single crust where possible.

Nutritional facts
● GI rating – Medium
● Calories – 216
● Protein – 3 g
● Carbohydrate – 25 g
● Fat – 13 g

Potatoes with garlic and pancetta

Preparation time 10 minutes
Cooking time 15 minutes

4 oz cubed pancetta

1 onion, chopped

1 1/4 lb potatoes, cooked and cubed

2 garlic cloves, crushed

1 tablespoon chopped parsley

2 tablespoons grated Parmesan cheese

1 Cook the pancetta in a nonstick skillet for 3–4 minutes until beginning to brown.

2 Add the onion, potatoes, and garlic and continue to fry for 8–10 minutes until the potatoes are browned, then stir in the parsley.

3 Place the mixture in a flameproof dish and sprinkle with the Parmesan. Cook under a preheated hot broiler for 1–2 minutes, until the Parmesan is melted and golden.

Nutritional tip
Eating a garlic clove a day is thought to be beneficial in promoting a healthy heart and lowering cholesterol.

Nutritional facts
- GI rating – Medium-High
- Calories – 246
- Protein – 13 g
- Carbohydrate – 28 g
- Fat – 8 g

Smoked mackerel and potato salad

Preparation time 10 minutes, plus cooling
Cooking time 15 minutes, plus standing

1 Cook the potatoes in a pan of lightly salted boiling water until tender. Drain, then toss them in the French dressing and allow to cool for 10 minutes.

2 When the potatoes are cool, gently stir in the cress, avocado, scallions, and smoked mackerel and serve.

2 lb baby new potatoes, halved

4 tablespoons fat-free French dressing

1 container cress, chopped

1 avocado, pitted and chopped

3 scallions, sliced

2 peppered smoked mackerel fillets, flaked

Nutritional tip
Avocados are high in monounsaturated fats, which are thought to lower blood cholesterol levels.

Nutritional facts
- GI rating – Medium
- Calories – 289
- Protein – 9 g
- Carbohydrate – 20 g
- Fat – 18 g

Crushed new potatoes with herby salmon

Preparation time 10 minutes
Cooking time 20 minutes

1½ lb new potatoes

small piece of butter

grated zest and juice of
  2 limes

1 bunch of scallions, sliced

4 pieces boneless, skinless
  salmon fillet, about 4 oz
  each

4 tablespoons light sour cream

3 tablespoons chopped mixed
  herbs (such as parsley and
  dill weed)

salt and pepper

lime wedges, to garnish

1 Cook the potatoes in a pan of lightly salted boiling water until tender. Drain and lightly crush with a fork.

2 Stir in the butter, half of the lime zest and juice, and half of the scallions, and season with plenty of black pepper.

3 Place the salmon pieces on a foil-lined broiler pan and cook under a preheated moderate broiler for 6–7 minutes, turning halfway through cooking, or until the salmon is just cooked.

4 Mix together the remaining lime zest and juice, scallions, sour cream, and herbs. Serve the salmon with the potatoes and the herby sauce, garnished with lime wedges.

Nutritional tip
Potatoes are high in carbohydrates, protein, and fiber and are therefore very good for you. It is a myth that they are fattening; it is only when they are cooked in oil or when cream and butter are added that they become so.

Nutritional facts
- GI rating – Medium
- Calories – 350
- Protein – 45 g
- Carbohydrate – 31 g
- Fat – 8 g

Salmon fishcakes with tomato and pepper salsa

Preparation time 10 minutes
Cooking time 30 minutes

1 lb potatoes, chopped

grated zest and juice
 of 1 lemon

4 tablespoons milk

1 bunch of scallions, sliced

½ teaspoon cayenne pepper

2 x 7 oz cans salmon in water
 or brine, drained and flaked

2 tablespoons all-purpose
 flour

1 egg, beaten

2 cups fresh white bread
 crumbs

1 tablespoon olive oil

salt and pepper

SALSA

4 tomatoes, finely chopped

1 green chili, finely chopped

1 red bell pepper, cored,
 seeded, and finely chopped

grated zest and juice of 1 lime

2 tablespoons chopped parsley

1 Cook the potatoes in a pan of lightly salted boiling water until tender. Drain and mash.

2 Stir in the lemon zest and juice, milk, scallions, cayenne pepper, and the salmon. Season to taste with salt and pepper.

3 Form the mixture into 8 patties. Dip them in the flour, then the egg, and then the bread crumbs.

4 Place the fishcakes on a lightly oiled baking sheet and drizzle over the remaining oil. Cook in a preheated oven at 400°F for 12–15 minutes until golden and piping hot.

5 Meanwhile, mix together all the salsa ingredients. Serve the salsa with the fishcakes.

Nutritional tip
Red and orange fruit and vegetables are a good source of beta-carotene. This is an antioxidant that can protect against heart disease.

Nutritional facts
- **GI rating** – Medium
- **Calories** – 385
- **Protein** – 25 g
- **Carbohydrate** – 46 g
- **Fat** – 12 g

Hearty seafood soup

1 Melt the butter in a large saucepan, add the onion, bay leaf, celery, and potatoes and fry for 3–4 minutes.

2 Add the milk and fish stock, bring to a boil, cover, and simmer for 15–20 minutes, until the potatoes are cooked.

3 Add the fish, shrimp, peas, and corn to the pan and continue to simmer for an additional 5 minutes or until the fish is cooked through.

4 Season with salt and pepper, turn into a warmed tureen, and top with the parsley and the chopped tomatoes. Serve with bread.

1 tablespoon butter

1 onion, chopped

1 bay leaf

2 celery sticks, finely sliced

10 oz floury potatoes, cubed

1³⁄₄ cups skim milk

1³⁄₄ cups fish stock

12 oz mixed boneless, skinless fish fillets (such as smoked haddock, cod, and salmon), cubed

4 oz cooked peeled shrimp

²⁄₃ cup frozen peas

²⁄₃ cup frozen corn kernels

3 tablespoons chopped parsley

2 tomatoes, finely chopped

bread, to serve

Nutritional tip
Try to use unsaturated fat for cooking. Butter may be used in small amounts where flavor is important.

Nutritional facts
- **GI rating** – Medium
- **Calories** – 301
- **Protein** – 30 g
- **Carbohydrate** – 30 g
- **Fat** – 7 g

Lemon chicken with potato wedges and garlic

Preparation time 10 minutes
Cooking time 30 minutes

4 boneless, skinless chicken breasts

1 lb potatoes, cut into wedges and parboiled

4 garlic cloves

grated zest and juice of 1 lemon

1 tablespoon olive oil

$^2/_3$ cup chicken stock

2 tablespoons chopped oregano

salt and pepper

1 Cut 3 slits in each chicken breast, then place them in an ovenproof dish with the potatoes and garlic.

2 Mix together the lemon zest and juice, olive oil, and stock. Season with salt and pepper and pour over the chicken and potatoes.

3 Cover the dish with foil and bake in a preheated oven at 400°F for 25 minutes. Remove the foil and continue to cook for 5 minutes more.

4 When the chicken and potatoes are cooked through, sprinkle with the oregano and serve.

Nutritional tip
Use reduced-salt bouillon cubes or make your own stock to cut down on the amount of salt in your diet.

Nutritional facts
- GI rating – Medium-High
- Calories – 304
- Protein – 43 g
- Carbohydrate – 20 g
- Fat – 5 g

Mediterranean potato salad ⓥ

Preparation time 5 minutes
Cooking time 15 minutes, plus standing

1 Cook the potatoes in a saucepan of lightly salted boiling water until tender. Drain, then stir in the French dressing and add the sun-dried tomatoes.

2 Allow the potatoes to cool for 10 minutes. Stir in the olives, red onion, feta, and herbs and toss well. Serve warm.

2 lb small new potatoes

4 tablespoons fat-free French dressing

4 sun-dried tomatoes in oil, sliced

1/3 cup black olives, pitted

1 red onion, finely sliced

2 oz feta cheese, cubed

large bunch of herbs (such as parsley or basil), chopped

Nutritional tip
Olives and sun-dried tomatoes contain oil and salt, but you need to use only a small amount for a rich flavor.

Nutritional facts
- GI rating – Medium
- Calories – 266
- Protein – 7 g
- Carbohydrate – 44 g
- Fat – 8 g

Pan-fried calf's liver with mustard and sage mash

Preparation time 10 minutes
Cooking time 15 minutes

1½ lb potatoes, cubed
2 garlic cloves
6 tablespoons light sour cream
1 tablespoon chopped sage
4 slices of calf's liver, about 5 oz each
2 tablespoons seasoned flour
1 tablespoon olive oil
salt and pepper
gravy, to serve

1 Cook the potatoes and garlic in a saucepan of lightly salted boiling water for 10–12 minutes until tender, then drain.

2 Mash the potatoes and garlic with the sour cream and sage and season to taste with plenty of freshly ground black pepper.

3 Meanwhile, press the pieces of liver into the seasoned flour to coat them all over. Heat the oil in a nonstick skillet, add the liver, and fry for 1–2 minutes on each side or until cooked to your desire. Serve with the mash and gravy.

Nutritional tip
Liver is a good source of fat-soluble vitamin A, however you should avoid it if you are pregnant since excess vitamin A can be harmful to an unborn baby.

Nutritional facts
- **GI rating** – High
- **Calories** – 307
- **Protein** – 31 g
- **Carbohydrate** – 30 g
- **Fat** – 12 g

Tenderloin of pork with pear and potato

Preparation time 10 minutes
Cooking time 25 minutes

1 Make a few small cuts in the tenderloin with a sharp knife and push a sliver of garlic into each cut. Rub the pork all over with the seasoned flour.

2 Heat the oil in a skillet, add the pork, and fry for 3–4 minutes over a moderate heat until browned on all sides. Add the cider and simmer until reduced by half.

3 Transfer the pork and juices to a shallow ovenproof dish with the potatoes, pears, and thyme.

4 Bake the dish in a preheated oven at 400°F for 20 minutes or until the pork is cooked through and the potatoes are tender. Stir the sour cream through the cooking juices and season to taste with salt and pepper. Serve with steamed vegetables or a salad.

1 lb piece pork tenderloin
2 garlic cloves, cut into slivers
1 tablespoon seasoned flour
1 tablespoon oil
$2/3$ cup hard cider
1 lb new potatoes, parboiled
2 pears, quartered and cored
2 thyme sprigs
3 tablespoons light sour cream
salt and pepper
steamed vegetables or salad, to serve

Nutritional tip
Choose a lean piece of pork which is low in fat and remove any visible fat before cooking.

Nutritional facts
- GI rating – Medium
- Calories – 430
- Protein – 43 g
- Carbohydrate – 42 g
- Fat – 12 g

Extra fruit and vegetables

Warm eggplant salad ⓥ

1 Heat the oil in a nonstick skillet. Add the eggplants and fry for 10 minutes until golden and softened. Add the red onion, capers, tomatoes, parsley, and vinegar and stir to combine.

2 Remove the pan from the heat and allow to cool for 10 minutes. Serve the eggplant salad with salad leaves and crusty bread.

Preparation time 10 minutes, plus cooling
Cooking time 10 minutes

2 tablespoons olive oil

2 eggplants, cut into small cubes

1 red onion, finely sliced

2 tablespoons capers, roughly chopped

4 tomatoes, chopped

4 tablespoons chopped parsley

1 tablespoon balsamic vinegar

TO SERVE
salad leaves
fresh crusty bread

Nutritional tip
The purple color of eggplant skin is due to a type of anthocyanin, which acts as an antioxidant. The eggplant is also low in calories, however it does soak up oil, so be careful when cooking it.

Nutritional facts
- GI rating – Low
- Calories – 99
- Protein – 3 g
- Carbohydrate – 9 g
- Fat – 6 g

Coconut and butternut squash soup Ⓥ

Preparation time 10 minutes
Cooking time 20 minutes

1 tablespoon olive oil

1 onion, chopped

1 garlic clove, crushed

2 butternut squash, peeled, seeded, and cubed

2 teaspoons medium curry paste

2½ cups vegetable stock

¾ cup reduced-fat coconut milk

2 tablespoons chopped cilantro leaves

crusty bread, to serve

1 Heat the oil in a nonstick saucepan. Add the onion and garlic and fry for 4–5 minutes until softened.

2 Add the squash and continue to fry for 1 minute. Stir in the curry paste and fry for another minute.

3 Pour over the stock and bring to a boil. Cover the pan and simmer for 15 minutes, until the squash is tender.

4 Transfer the soup to a food processor or blender and blend until smooth. Return it to the pan, add the coconut milk and cilantro, stir, and season to taste with salt and pepper. Heat through, then serve with plenty of crusty bread.

Nutritional tip
Butternut squash is a nutritious, starchy root vegetable which can be used as an alternative to potatoes.

Nutritional facts
- **GI rating** – Medium
- **Calories** – 120
- **Protein** – 2 g
- **Carbohydrate** – 18 g
- **Fat** – 4 g

Bacon, spinach, and blue cheese salad

1 Fry the bacon in a nonstick skillet until crisp. Add the pine nuts and continue to cook for 1–2 minutes until the nuts are beginning to brown.

2 Toss together the spinach, Gorgonzola, and tomatoes, then stir these into the bacon and pine nuts. Place the salad in a serving bowl.

3 Mix together the dressing ingredients and drizzle over the salad. Serve with crusty bread.

Preparation time 10 minutes
Cooking time 5 minutes

3 Canadian bacon slices, chopped

3 tablespoons pine nuts

4$\frac{1}{2}$ cups baby spinach leaves

2 oz Gorgonzola cheese, cubed

12 cherry tomatoes, halved

crusty bread, to serve

DRESSING

1 teaspoon wholegrain mustard

2 tablespoons balsamic vinegar

1 teaspoon honey

Nutritional tip
Although honey is high in sugar it can be used in small amounts in dressings and in cooking to add sweetness and flavor.

Nutritional facts
- GI rating – Medium
- Calories – 146
- Protein – 8 g
- Carbohydrate – 5 g
- Fat – 16 g

Charred asparagus with parmesan Ⓥ

Preparation time 5 minutes
Cooking time 5 minutes

8 oz asparagus tips
2 teaspoons olive oil
1 oz Parmesan cheese shavings
pepper

1 Place the asparagus on a baking sheet and drizzle over the oil. Place under a preheated hot broiler and cook for 3–4 minutes, turning occasionally, until tender and beginning to char.

2 Serve the asparagus with the Parmesan shavings and plenty of black pepper sprinkled over the top.

Nutritional tip
Asparagus is a source of fructo-oligosaccharides (FOS), a type of fiber that promotes the growth of healthy bacteria in the gut.

Nutritional facts
- GI rating – Low-Medium
- Calories – 93
- Protein – 4 g
- Carbohydrate – 1 g
- Fat – 7 g

Broiled spiced butternut squash ⓥ

Preparation time 10 minutes
Cooking time 15 minutes

2 butternut squash, peeled, seeded, and cubed
1 tablespoon coriander seeds
1 tablespoon cumin seeds
1 tablespoon paprika
2 tablespoons olive oil
2 tablespoons chopped cilantro leaves
4 tablespoons plain yogurt

1 Place the squash in a pan of boiling water and simmer for 5 minutes. Drain and place on a baking sheet.

2 Put the coriander seeds and cumin seeds into a small pan and heat for 1 minute until the spices become fragrant, then crush them using a mortar and pestle.

3 Combine the crushed seed mixture, paprika, and olive oil. Drizzle over the squash, then place under a preheated hot broiler for 8–10 minutes, until tender and beginning to char.

4 Mix together the chopped cilantro and yogurt and serve with the spiced squash.

Nutritional tip
Butternut squash is an excellent source of beta-carotene, which can be converted by the body into vitamin A.

Nutritional facts
- **GI rating** – Medium-High
- **Calories** – 155
- **Protein** – 5 g
- **Carbohydrate** – 13 g
- **Fat** – 9 g

Summer vegetable salad Ⓥ

Preparation time 10 minutes, plus marinating
Cooking time 1 minute

2 zucchini

2 carrots

5 oz snow peas, halved lengthwise

1 red bell pepper, cored, seeded, and sliced

1½ cups bean sprouts

1 red chili, finely sliced

4 tablespoons chopped cilantro leaves

2 tablespoons sesame seeds, toasted

1 tablespoon sesame oil

grated zest and juice of 1 lime

1 Use a vegetable peeler to slice the zucchini and the carrots into fine ribbons. Place them in a pan of boiling water, then immediately drain and refresh under cold running water.

2 Toss the zucchini and carrot ribbons with the snow peas, red pepper, bean sprouts, chili, cilantro, sesame seeds, oil, and lime zest and juice. Set aside for 20 minutes to allow the flavors to infuse. Serve in a large bowl.

Nutritional tip
Chilies owe their heat to the phytochemical capsaicin, which is concentrated in the seeds and can help relieve nasal congestion. They are also rich in vitamin C.

Nutritional facts
- GI rating – Medium
- Calories – 116
- Protein – 5 g
- Carbohydrate – 7 g
- Fat – 7 g

Garlic mushrooms with wilted spinach and crispy bacon

Preparation time 10 minutes
Cooking time 10 minutes

8 open-cap mushrooms

4 tablespoons water

³/₄ cup extra-light garlic and herb cream cheese

grated zest of 1 lemon

2 cups baby leaf spinach

4 Canadian bacon slices, broiled until crisp, then roughly chopped

salt and pepper

1 Place the mushrooms, gill sides up, in a large nonstick skillet with the water.

2 Mix together the cream cheese and lemon zest, then season to taste with salt and pepper. Divide the mixture between the mushroom caps. Cover and cook over a low heat for 5–6 minutes.

3 Layer the spinach over the mushrooms, cover the pan, and continue to cook for 2 minutes, until the spinach has wilted.

4 Divide the mushrooms between warmed serving plates, then top with the bacon and serve.

Nutritional tip
Look out for the different levels of fat in cream cheese—extra-light is low-fat and light is medium-fat.

Nutritional facts
- **GI rating** – Low
- **Calories** – 93
- **Protein** – 5 g
- **Carbohydrate** – 0 g
- **Fat** – 8 g

Eggplant and mozzarella stacks with pesto dressing Ⓥ

Preparation time 10 minutes
Cooking time 20 minutes

2 eggplants, each sliced into 12 rounds
1 tablespoon olive oil
16 basil leaves
4 tomatoes, each cut into 4 slices
5 oz mozzarella cheese, cut into 8 slices
arugula leaves, to serve

DRESSING
1 tablespoon pesto
1 tablespoon balsamic vinegar

1 Brush the eggplant slices with a little oil. Place them on a broiler pan and cook under a preheated hot broiler for 2–3 minutes on each side until beginning to brown.

2 Place 8 slices of eggplant on a baking sheet and top each one with a basil leaf, a slice of tomato, and a slice of mozzarella. Place another piece of eggplant on top of each stack, then another slice of tomato, a basil leaf, and finally another slice of eggplant.

3 Cook in a preheated oven at 400°F for 15 minutes, until golden and tender.

4 Mix together the dressing ingredients. Serve the eggplant stacks on a bed of arugula, and drizzle with the dressing.

Nutritional tip
As well as being one of the most popular of salad vegetables, tomatoes are a source of vitamins C and E, potassium, and beta-carotene.

Nutritional facts
- **GI rating** – Medium
- **Calories** – 157
- **Protein** – 7 g
- **Carbohydrate** – 9 g
- **Fat** – 10 g

Fresh figs with ricotta cheese and parma ham

Preparation time 10 minutes

8 fresh figs
1 teaspoon Dijon mustard
$\frac{1}{2}$ cup ricotta cheese
3 oz Parma ham, thinly sliced
2 tablespoons balsamic vinegar
salt and pepper
crusty bread, to serve

1 Cut the figs into 4, leaving them attached at the base.

2 Stir the mustard into the ricotta and season to taste with salt and pepper.

3 Divide the ricotta mixture between the figs, spooning it over the top. Place two figs on each serving plate and top with some slices of Parma ham.

4 Drizzle over the balsamic vinegar and serve the figs with crusty bread.

Nutritional tip
Both fresh figs and dried figs are a good source of antioxidant vitamins, fiber, and potassium.

Nutritional facts
- GI rating – Low
- Calories – 139
- Protein – 10 g
- Carbohydrate – 11 g
- Fat – 6 g

Vegetable curry ⓥ

Preparation time 10 minutes
Cooking time 25 minutes

1 Heat the oil in a large saucepan, add the onion and garlic and fry for 2 minutes. Stir in the curry paste and fry for 1 minute more.

2 Add the vegetables and fry for 2–3 minutes, stirring occasionally, then add the tomatoes and coconut milk. Stir well and bring to a boil, then lower the heat and simmer for 12–15 minutes until all the vegetables are cooked.

3 Stir the cilantro leaves into the curry and serve with rice.

1 tablespoon olive oil

1 onion, chopped

1 garlic clove, crushed

2 tablespoons medium curry paste

3 lb prepared mixed vegetables (such as green beans, zucchini, bell peppers, squash, and mushrooms)

7 oz can chopped tomatoes

1$\frac{3}{4}$ cups reduced-fat coconut milk

2 tablespoons chopped cilantro leaves

boiled rice, to serve

Nutritional tip
Transform this vegetable curry into a well-balanced meal with the addition of rice and an Indian bread.

Nutritional facts
- GI rating – Medium
- Calories – 172
- Protein – 6 g
- Carbohydrate – 26 g
- Fat – 5 g

Baked red fruits with crispy topping Ⓥ

Preparation time 5 minutes
Cooking time 20 minutes

2 lb mixed summer berries
(such as strawberries,
raspberries, and blackberries)

grated zest and juice
of 1 orange

TOPPING

$^3/_4$ cup crunchy oat cereal

$^3/_4$ cup rolled oats

2 tablespoons melted butter

1 tablespoon honey

3 tablespoons chopped
hazelnuts

1 Place the fruits, orange zest, and juice in an ovenproof dish.

2 Cook in a preheated oven at 400°F for 10 minutes until the juices begin to run.

3 Mix together all the topping ingredients and sprinkle over the fruits.

4 Return the dish to the oven and cook for an additional 10 minutes until the topping is bubbling and golden.

Nutritional tip
Rolled oats are high in soluble fiber and have a low glycemic index. Oatmeal is a useful snack food.

Nutritional facts
- GI rating – Medium
- Calories – 331
- Protein – 8 g
- Carbohydrate – 50 g
- Fat – 12 g

Griddled pineapple and ginger Ⓥ

Preparation time 5 minutes
Cooking time 5 minutes

2 tablespoons confectioners' sugar

1 teaspoon ground ginger

1 pineapple, peeled and cut into 1 inch thick rounds

4 tablespoons virtually fat-free yogurt, to serve

1 Heat a griddle or a heavy skillet until hot.

2 Mix together the confectioners' sugar and ginger and sprinkle over both sides of the pineapple rings. Place the pineapple on the griddle and cook for 1–2 minutes on each side until golden.

3 Serve the pineapple hot with the yogurt.

Nutritional tip
Pineapple contains bromelain, an enzyme which breaks down protein.

Nutritional facts
- **GI rating** – Medium-High
- **Calories** – 107
- **Protein** – 4 g
- **Carbohydrate** – 23 g
- **Fat** – 0 g

Tropical fruit salad Ⓥ

Preparation time 15 minutes, plus standing

1 Combine all the ingredients in a large serving bowl, cover, and leave in the refrigerator for 20 minutes for the flavors to develop.

1 melon, seeded and cubed

14 oz can pineapple cubes in natural juice, drained and juice reserved

2 kiwifruits, sliced

1 papaya, cubed

4 tablespoons lime juice

2 pieces preserved ginger in syrup, finely chopped, plus 2 tablespoons of the syrup

pulp and seeds of 2 passion fruits

Nutritional tip
One kiwifruit contains the recommended daily allowance of vitamin C.

Nutritional facts
- **GI rating** – Medium-High
- **Calories** – 94
- **Protein** – 2 g
- **Carbohydrate** – 22 g
- **Fat** – 0 g

Watermelon granita Ⓥ

Preparation time 10 minutes, plus freezing

1 watermelon, seeded, cubed, and frozen

grated zest and juice of 1 lime

2 tablespoons confectioners' sugar

1 Place all the ingredients in a food processor or blender and blend until smooth.

2 Serve immediately in frosted glasses.

Nutritional tip
To reduce the sugar content of this recipe use granulated intense sweetener instead of confectioners' sugar.

Nutritional facts
- GI rating – High
- Calories – 92
- Protein – 1 g
- Carbohydrate – 22 g
- Fat – 1 g

Individual lime and raspberry cheesecakes Ⓥ

Preparation time 10 minutes

6 ginger cookies, lightly crushed

³/₄ cup extra-light cream cheese

³/₄ cup virtually fat-free yogurt

few drops of vanilla extract

1 tablespoon superfine sugar

grated zest and juice of 1 lime

1 cup raspberries

lime wedges, to garnish

1 Divide the cookies between 4 small glass dishes.

2 In a bowl, mix together the cream cheese, yogurt, vanilla extract, sugar, and lime zest and juice.

3 Spoon the mixture over the cookies, then top with the raspberries. Serve immediately garnished with a lime wedge.

Nutritional tip
Choose very fresh raspberries as they have a higher antioxidant content and are more nutritious.

Nutritional facts
- GI rating – Medium-High
- Calories – 180
- Protein – 8 g
- Carbohydrate – 23 g
- Fat – 7 g

Broiled nectarines with mint vanilla cream Ⓥ

Preparation time 10 minutes
Cooking time 7-8 minutes

4 nectarines, halved and pitted
pinch of ground cinnamon
1 tablespoon honey
grated zest and juice
    of 1 orange
4 tablespoons light sour cream
$^2/_3$ cup plain yogurt
1 tablespoon chopped mint
few drops of vanilla extract

1 Place the nectarines on a broiler pan, cut side up. Mix together the cinnamon, honey, and orange zest and juice, and drizzle over the nectarines.

2 Place the nectarines under a preheated hot broiler and cook for 7-8 minutes until golden, basting occasionally with the juices.

3 Mix together the sour cream, yogurt, mint, and vanilla extract and serve with the nectarines.

Nutritional tip
Plain yogurt is low in fat and can be used in sweet and savory dishes.

Nutritional facts
- GI rating – Medium
- Calories – 108
- Protein – 4 g
- Carbohydrate – 23 g
- Fat – 3 g

Super smoothies ⓥ

1 Place all the ingredients in a food processor or blender and blend until smooth.

2 Serve in tall glasses.

STRAWBERRY
1 banana, chopped
3 cups strawberries, hulled
3³/₄ cups ice-cold low-fat milk

PEACH MELBA
1 banana, chopped
2 peaches, pitted
1¹/₂ cups strawberries, hulled
3³/₄ cups ice-cold low-fat milk

TROPICAL
1 lb frozen tropical fruits, almost defrosted
2¹/₂ cups ice-cold unsweetened pineapple juice

Nutritional tip
Smoothies are packed with vitamins and fiber and a good way of consuming the recommended daily allowance of fruit.

Nutritional facts
- GI rating – Medium

Strawberry
- Calories – 158
- Protein – 9 g
- Carbohydrate – 25 g
- Fat – 3 g

Peach melba
- Calories – 159
- Protein – 9 g
- Carbohydrate – 25 g
- Fat – 3 g

Tropical
- Calories – 105
- Protein – 1 g
- Carbohydrate – 27 g
- Fat – 0 g

Bread as a basis

Baked tortillas with hummus Ⓥ

Preparation time 5 minutes
Cooking time 12 minutes

4 small flour tortillas
1 tablespoon olive oil

HUMMUS
13 oz can chickpeas, drained
  and rinsed
1 garlic clove
4 tablespoons thick yogurt
2 tablespoons lemon juice
1 tablespoon chopped cilantro
  leaves
salt and pepper
paprika, to serve
cilantro sprig, to garnish

1 Cut each tortilla into 8 triangles, arrange on a baking sheet, and brush with a little oil. Place in a preheated oven at 400°F and bake for 10–12 minutes until golden and crisp. Allow to cool.

2 Meanwhile, put all the ingredients for the hummus, except the paprika and cilantro, in a food processor or blender and blend until almost smooth.

3 Season to taste with salt and pepper, stir in the cilantro, and sprinkle with paprika. Garnish with a cilantro sprig and serve with the tortilla chips.

Nutritional tip
Store-bought tortilla chips and hummus are high in fat. This recipe is a delicious low-fat alternative.

Nutritional facts
- **GI rating** – Low
- **Calories** – 306
- **Protein** – 12 g
- **Carbohydrate** – 46 g
- **Fat** – 9 g

Pita with citrus chicken brochettes

Preparation time 10 minutes, plus standing
Cooking time 10 minutes

3 boneless, skinless chicken breasts, cubed

1 teaspoon chopped thyme

grated zest and juice of 1 orange

grated zest and juice of 1 lime

1 red bell pepper, cored, seeded, and cubed

1 onion, cut into wedges

4 large pita breads

1$\frac{1}{2}$ cups salad leaves

4 tablespoons thick yogurt

1 tablespoon chopped mint

1 Place the chicken cubes in a nonmetallic dish with the chopped thyme, orange and lemon zest and juice, and allow to marinate for 10 minutes.

2 Divide the chicken, red pepper, and onion between 8 wooden barbecue skewers.

3 Place the brochettes under a preheated moderate broiler for 7–8 minutes, turning occasionally and brushing with a little marinade from time to time, until browned and cooked through.

4 Warm the pitas and slit along one side to make a pocket. Fill with the salad leaves and the brochettes.

5 Mix together the yogurt and mint and spoon into the pitas. Serve hot.

Nutritional tip
Served with plenty of salad, these pitas are a complete meal.

Nutritional facts
- GI rating – Medium
- Calories – 437
- Protein – 42 g
- Carbohydrate – 53 g
- Fat – 7 g

108 bread as a basis

Italian bread salad ⓥ

Preparation time 5 minutes, plus standing
Cooking time 5 minutes

1 Put the bread on a broiler pan in one layer, place under a preheated moderate broiler and toast until golden all over.

2 In a large bowl, mix the bread with tomatoes, cucumber, capers, red onion, olives, basil, and French dressing. Season with black pepper and set aside for 10 minutes to allow the flavors to develop. Serve at room temperature.

1 ciabatta loaf, torn into bite-size pieces

4 tomatoes, cut into chunks

$\frac{1}{2}$ cucumber, chopped

3 tablespoons capers, drained

1 red onion, finely sliced

24 black olives, pitted

handful of basil, torn

4 tablespoons virtually fat-free French dressing

pepper

Nutritional tip
Olives contain natural antioxidants called polyphenols, they are also a good source of vitamin E.

Nutritional facts
- GI rating – Medium
- Calories – 236
- Protein – 8 g
- Carbohydrate – 44 g
- Fat – 4 g

Steak sandwiches

Preparation time 10 minutes, plus standing

Cooking time 8 minutes

1 Heat a griddle or nonstick skillet until very hot.

2 Place the steak on the griddle and cook for 2 minutes on each side, or until cooked to taste. Remove the steak and leave it to rest for 5 minutes.

3 Meanwhile, add the oil to the griddle and fry the sliced onion for 2–3 minutes.

4 Mix together the sour cream and mustard.

5 Assemble the sandwich by placing the steak in the bread, then add the arugula, tomatoes, and onion. Finish with a dollop of the mustard and sour cream mixture and season to taste with salt and pepper.

4 pieces thin cut sirloin steak, about 4 oz each

1 tablespoon oil

1 onion, sliced

4 tablespoons light sour cream

1 tablespoon wholegrain mustard

1 French stick, cut into 4 and split down one side

1 1/2 cups arugula

2 tomatoes, sliced

salt and pepper

Nutritional tip
Lean steak is full of nutrients and minerals. It also makes a low-fat sandwich filling.

Nutritional facts
- **GI rating** – Medium
- **Calories** – 388
- **Protein** – 30 g
- **Carbohydrate** – 46 g
- **Fat** – 12 g

Tasty open toasties

Preparation time 5 minutes
Cooking time 15 minutes

1 Toast the bread on both sides, then top each piece with a slice of ham and 2 tomato slices.

2 To poach the eggs, bring a large saucepan of water to a boil, add the vinegar, then stir the water rapidly in a circular motion to create a whirlpool. Break an egg into the center of the pan to allow the white to wrap around the yolk. Cook for 3 minutes then remove from the pan and keep warm. Repeat with the remaining eggs, then place 1 egg on each piece of toast.

3 Mix together the sour cream and herbs, season to taste with salt and pepper, and serve with the toasties.

4 thick slices of multigrain bread

4 slices of lean ham

2 tomatoes, sliced

4 eggs

1 tablespoon white wine vinegar

3 tablespoons light sour cream

2 tablespoons chopped herbs (such as parsley or tarragon)

salt and pepper

Nutritional tip
Multigrain bread has additional whole-wheat grains added to the mixture, making it rougher in texture and lower in glycemic index.

Nutritional facts
- GI rating – Medium
- Calories – 212
- Protein – 14 g
- Carbohydrate – 21 g
- Fat – 11 g

Chicken fajitas

Preparation time 10 minutes
Cooking time 10 minutes

1 Heat the oil in a skillet, add the chicken, and fry for 2–3 minutes until beginning to brown.

2 Add the onions, bell peppers, and pepper flakes and continue to fry for 5 minutes more. Remove from the heat and stir in the cilantro and lime juice.

3 Warm the tortillas according to the package instructions, then fill them with the chicken mixture and sour cream. Garnish with cilantro sprigs and serve with salad leaves.

1 tablespoon olive oil

2 boneless, skinless chicken breasts, sliced

2 red onions, cut into wedges

2 red bell peppers, cored, seeded, and sliced

1 yellow bell pepper, cored, seeded, and sliced

pinch of dried red pepper flakes

2 tablespoons chopped cilantro leaves

2 tablespoons lime juice

8 medium flour tortillas

4 tablespoons light sour cream

cilantro sprigs, to garnish

1 ½ cups salad leaves, to serve

Nutritional tip
Chicken is full of vitamins and minerals and with the skin removed it is also low in fat.

Nutritional facts
- **GI rating** – Medium
- **Calories** – 328
- **Protein** – 26 g
- **Carbohydrate** – 46 g
- **Fat** – 7 g

Grilled chicken sandwich

Preparation time 5 minutes
Cooking time 10 minutes

1 tablespoon oil

1 onion, sliced

2 boneless, skinless chicken breasts, sliced

2 tablespoons plain yogurt

1 French stick, quartered and split along one side

1½ cups arugula

salt and pepper

1 Heat the oil in a nonstick skillet, add the onion, and fry for 2–3 minutes, until beginning to soften.

2 Add the chicken to the pan and continue to fry for 4–5 minutes, until the chicken is browned and cooked through. Stir in the yogurt and season well with black pepper.

3 Fill the bread with the chicken and arugula and serve.

Nutritional tip
Always remove the skin from chicken before cooking to reduce the fat content.

Nutritional facts
- GI rating – Medium
- Calories – 256
- Protein – 26 g
- Carbohydrate – 27 g
- Fat – 5 g

Smoked haddock and poached egg muffins

Preparation time 10 minutes
Cooking time 20 minutes

4 pieces skinless, natural smoked haddock, about 4 oz each

1 1/4 cups milk

1 bay leaf

2 peppercorns

1 tablespoon white wine vinegar

4 eggs

1 1/2 cups arugula

4 English breakfast muffins, halved and toasted

4 tablespoons reduced-fat hollandaise sauce

pepper

1 Place the fish in a large skillet, pour over the milk, and add the bay leaf and peppercorns. Bring to a boil, then simmer gently for 4–5 minutes, until the fish is just cooked.

2 Bring another pan of water to a boil and add the vinegar. Stir the water rapidly in a circular motion to create a whirlpool. Break an egg into the center of the pan to allow the white to wrap around the yolk. Cook for 3 minutes then remove from the pan and keep warm. Repeat with the remaining eggs.

3 Place a few arugula leaves on the bottom half of each muffin, and top with a piece of fish and a poached egg.

4 Spoon over the hollandaise, sprinkle with pepper, and serve topped with the other muffin half.

Nutritional tip
Smoked haddock is high in sodium but cooking it in a liquid such as milk helps to reduce the sodium content.

Nutritional facts
- **GI rating** – Medium-High
- **Calories** – 433
- **Protein** – 36 g
- **Carbohydrate** – 39 g
- **Fat** – 14 g

Smoked salmon blinis with dill cream

Preparation time 5 minutes
Cooking time 5 minutes

8 large blinis

2 tablespoons light sour cream

1 teaspoon chopped dill weed

grated zest of 1 lemon

2 scallions, sliced

4 oz smoked salmon

lemon wedges, to garnish

pepper

1 Gently warm the blinis for a few minutes under a broiler or in the oven.

2 Stir together the sour cream, dill, lemon zest, and scallions and season with pepper. Spoon the mixture onto the blinis and top with the salmon. Garnish with lemon wedges and serve.

Nutritional tip
Light sour cream is lower in fat than light cream and has around half the fat of standard sour cream.

Nutritional facts
- GI rating – Medium
- Calories – 171
- Protein – 9 g
- Carbohydrate – 20 g
- Fat – 8 g

Sardines on ciabatta with lime cream

Preparation time 5 minutes, plus marinating

Cooking time 5 minutes

8 sardines

grated zest and juice of 1 lemon

1 garlic clove, crushed

1 rosemary sprig, lightly bruised

1 tablespoon olive oil

LIME CREAM

4 tablespoons light sour cream

grated zest and juice of ½ lime

2 tablespoons chopped herbs

TO SERVE

1 ciabatta loaf, halved then split horizontally, to make 4 pieces

1 garlic clove, halved

1 Place the sardines in a nonmetallic dish with the lemon zest and juice, crushed garlic, rosemary, and oil. Cover and set aside for 15 minutes.

2 Mix together the ingredients for the lime cream.

3 Place the sardines on a broiler pan and cook under a preheated hot broiler for 4–5 minutes, turning halfway through cooking and brushing with a little of the marinade.

4 Toast the ciabatta, then rub each piece with the cut side of the garlic clove.

5 Serve the sardines on the ciabatta with the lime cream on the side.

Nutritional tip
Sardines are oily fish which are high in fat-soluble vitamins and Omega-3 fatty acids, which are thought to protect against heart disease.

Nutritional facts
- GI rating – Medium
- Calories – 337
- Protein – 30 g
- Carbohydrate – 22 g
- Fat – 15 g

Smoked mackerel pâté on toast

7 oz peppered smoked mackerel fillets, skinned

$^3/_4$ cup extra-light cream cheese

1 tablespoon horseradish cream

2 tablespoons light sour cream

hot toast, to serve

1 Place the mackerel, cream cheese, horseradish, and sour cream in a food processor or blender and blend until almost smooth.

2 Serve the pâté with plenty of hot toast.

Nutritional tip
Extra-light cream cheese is low in fat and ideal for making pâtés.

Nutritional facts
- **GI rating** – Medium
- **Calories** – 274
- **Protein** – 14 g
- **Carbohydrate** – 3 g
- **Fat** – 19 g

Irish soda bread Ⓥ

Preparation time 15 minutes
Cooking time 30 minutes

1 Sift together the two flours, baking soda, and cream of tartar, then blend in the butter until the mixture resembles fine bread crumbs.

2 Quickly stir in the buttermilk and mix until a soft dough is formed.

3 Turn the dough onto a lightly floured work surface and knead until smooth.

4 Shape the dough into a round and place on a lightly floured baking sheet. Cut a cross in the top with a sharp knife, sprinkle with a little flour, then bake in a preheated oven at 400°F for 25–30 minutes.

1 1/2 cups all-purpose whole-wheat flour

1 3/4 cups all-purpose white flour, plus extra for dusting

1/2 teaspoon baking soda

1/2 teaspoon cream of tartar

2 tablespoons butter

1 1/4 cups buttermilk or skim milk

Nutritional tip
Whole-wheat flour is made from milling the whole wheat grain and is high in fiber.

Nutritional facts
- **GI rating** – Medium
- **Calories** – 1752
- **Protein** – 60 g
- **Carbohydrate** – 330 g
- **Fat** – 30 g

Glossary

Acarotenoid See Beta-carotene.

Anthocyanins Red, blue, and violet pigments in fruits like berries which act as antioxidants.

Antioxidants Substances that neutralize free radicals—substances that can cause damage to cells—in the body. They include vitamins C and E, carotenoids, and minerals like selenium.

Beta-carotene (acarotenoid) An orange or yellow pigment in fruits and vegetables that acts as an antioxidant and is converted in the body into vitamin A.

Blood glucose level The amount of sugar glucose in a person's bloodstream at any one time.

Bromelain An enzyme found in pineapple that helps in the digestion of protein.

Calories See Energy.

Carbohydrate Sugars and starches in food.

Carotenoids Red, yellow, and orange pigments in fruits and vegetables that act as antioxidants and are converted to vitamin A in the body.

CHO Short for carbohydrate.

Cholesterol A type of fat found in some foods, e.g. liver, eggs, and shellfish. High levels of cholesterol in the blood increase the risk of heart disease, but eating a diet high in saturated fat, being overweight, and not being physically active will raise your blood cholesterol levels more than eating foods high in cholesterol.

Complications Diabetes can lead to complications including cardiovascular disease (heart disease, stroke, and circulatory problems that can lead to amputation), nephropathy (damage to the blood vessels in the kidney that can lead to kidney failure), neuropathy (resulting in damage to the nerves), and retinopathy (damage to the blood vessels in the back of the eye that can lead to blindness).

Dietary guidelines A set of guidelines relating to the types and amounts of foods that a person should eat to maintain good health. Individuals with diabetes need to have dietary guidelines tailored specifically to their medical needs and lifestyle.

Dietitian See State Registered Dietitian.

Energy In dietary terms, this refers to the fuel a food provides for the body to use. Energy is usually measured in calories.

Enzymes Specialized proteins that control chemical reactions in the body. They are very important; their functions range from controlling the breakdown of food in the gut to helping to send messages to the inside of cells.

Fiber Indigestible components of carbohydrate that help maintain a healthy gut.

Flavonols Nutrients that act as antioxidants.

Folate One of the B vitamins. It is found in a variety of foods, including green leafy vegetables, nuts, grains, and liver.

Fructo-oligosaccharide (FOS) A type of fiber found in food that promotes the growth of healthy bacteria in the gut.

Genetics The study of inherited information.

Glucose A simple sugar that is found in some sweet foods, but which can also be derived from the breakdown of starchy foods as they are digested. Glucose in the bloodstream provides the muscles and organs of the body with energy.

Glycemic index (GI) A way of ranking foods containing carbohydrate, e.g. bread and sugar. High GI foods raise blood glucose levels quickly, while low GI foods raise blood glucose levels more slowly and can help to make them easier to manage if you have diabetes.

Glycogen The form in which glucose is stored in the body.

Gut Another name for the alimentary canal, which extends from the esophagus to the anus.

Hyperglycemia Abnormally high levels of sugar or glucose in the blood leading to increased thirst and urination, as well as vomiting. It can sometimes eventually lead to diabetic coma. Hyperglycemia can be treated by an insulin injection in order to lower the blood glucose level to the normal range (4–7mmol/l).

Hypoglycemia (hypo) Abnormally low levels of sugar or glucose in the blood, leading to trembling, cold sweats, headaches, confusion, and sometimes erratic behavior. A hypo should be treated by eating or drinking some form of sugar immediately in order to raise the blood glucose level to the normal range (4–7mmol/l).

Insulin A hormone produced by the pancreas that helps the body's cells to use glucose and also in maintaining normal levels of glucose in the blood.

Isoflavones Plant chemicals, found in soy beans which can have mild estrogen-like effects and can be beneficial in relieving menopausal symptoms, lowering cholesterol levels, and in the management of some cancers.

Lycopene A red pigment found in tomatoes which acts like an antioxidant.

Monounsaturated fats Types of unsaturated fats found in olive oil and canola oil, nuts, and avocados.

Omega-3 fatty acids Essential fatty acids that have been shown to reduce the risk of heart disease. They are found in oily fish such as halibut, trout, salmon, pilchards, sardines, and herrings.

Pancreas The gland where insulin is produced. It lies just behind the stomach.

Phytochemicals Plant chemicals which help protect against heart disease.

Polyphenols Natural antioxidant substances, found in olives, red wine, and nuts.

Polyunsaturated fats Fats found in oily fish, sunflower oil, corn oil, safflower oil, and a wide variety of margarines and spreads.

Proteins Composed of amino acids, these are a major component of body tissues, enzymes, and hormones and act as carriers in blood and body fluids.

Registered Dietitian A professional who can give you specific advice on your diet, based on your own personal needs and lifestyle.

Saturated fat A type of fat found in fatty meats and full-fat dairy products like whole milk, cheese, and cream. A diet rich in saturated fats increases the levels of cholesterol in the blood and can therefore increase the risk of heart disease.

Sodium An essential nutrient which we obtain mostly from salt in food like bread, canned and packaged foods, or when it is added as a flavoring. Only small amounts of sodium are needed to maintain health—too much of it in the diet is associated with raised blood pressure.

Soluble fiber Found in oats, legumes, fruits, and vegetables, soluble fiber can help people with diabetes to manage blood glucose levels and reduces fat levels in the blood.

Starchy foods Foods such as potatoes, rice, pasta, bread, and cereals.

Type 1 diabetes Also known as insulin dependent diabetes mellitus, IDDM, which develops when the body stops producing insulin. More common in younger people.

Type 2 diabetes Also known as non insulin dependent diabetes mellitus, NIDDM, which develops when the body is unable to produce enough insulin, or the insulin that it does produce is not working properly. More common in older people.

Unsaturated fats Fats found in oily fish, vegetables, and vegetable oils, which can be divided into monounsaturated fats and polyunsaturated fats.

Index

Acknowledgments

Executive Editor: Nicola Hill
Editor: Alice Bowden
Executive Art Editor: Leigh Jones
Designer: Tony Truscott
Production Controller: Ian Paton
Special Photography: William Reavell
Food Stylist: Louise Tyler
Dietitian: Norma McGough
Diabetes UK Publishing Manager: Clare Lemon

Picture credits:
Diabetes UK 24
Getty Telegraph 23 top
Octopus Publishing Group Limited/Stephen Conroy 19 bottom/David Jordan
17 right, 19 center right/William Reavell front cover top left, front cover top
right, front cover top center, front cover bottom left, front cover bottom right,
front cover bottom center, back cover top left, back cover bottom right,
title/William Reavell 6-7, 8, 11, 12, 13, 14, 15 top, 15 top center, 15 center,
15 center below, 15 bottom, 16 bottom, 17 left, 18, 19 left, 19 top, 19 center
2, 19 center 3, 19 bottom center, 20 top, 20 center, 20 bottom, 20 center
above, 20 center below, 21 top, 21 bottom, 21 center below, 21 center above,
21 center 1, 21 center 2, 22, 23 bottom right, 25, 28-29, 31, 35, 39, 43, 47, 49,
51, 53, 54-55, 59, 63, 67, 71, 73, 74-75, 79, 83, 88-89, 91, 93, 94-95, 99, 103,
107, 111, 115, 117, 119, 120-121, 123, 127, 129, 133, 137/Gareth Sambidge 10
right/Ian Wallace 16 top, 23 bottom left/Philip Webb 17 center, 19 center
Photodisc 9 right, 10 left, 19 top center, 19 center 1